The American Party

The American Party

Robert D. Mailho

iUniverse, Inc.
New York   Bloomington   Shanghai

The American Party

Copyright © 2008 by Robert D. Mailho

iUniverse books may be ordered through booksellers or by contacting:

iUniverse
1663 Liberty Drive
Bloomington, IN 47403
www.iuniverse.com
1-800-Authors (1-800-288-4677)

Because of the dynamic nature of the Internet, any Web addresses or links contained in this book may have changed since publication and may no longer be valid.

ISBN: 978-0-595-52090-9 (pbk)
ISBN: 978-0-595-61250-5 (ebk)

Printed in the United States of America

ROBERT DWIGHT MAILHO

My name is Bob Mailho, and I would like to introduce myself to you.

Birthplace:

Berkeley, California in 1935.

My parents:

My father, Emil P. Mailho, a professional baseball player for 18 years.
On August 13, 2006, during an A's game at McAfee Coliseum, the Oakland A's
honored him as one of the oldest living members of their team.
He had a batting average of .318.
My father passed away on March 7, 2007.
My mother, Lola S. (Silva) Mailho, a school teacher and homemaker.

Religion:

My father was a Catholic and my mother was Christian Scientist–what a mix!
I played organ at my Mother's Church at the age of 7 years old. I attended places
of worship of many of the religious faiths. I was fortunate to have parents
who let me go to all the churches, temples and mosques.

Early Schooling:

I was not a good student. I was always interrupting the class
asking "why" and "why not?"
So my teachers would send me to the Principal's Office. After
sitting in his office on
many occasions, he asked me if I would like to go to the library.
After my first visit to
the library, I knew that this room was my real class room. The
Librarian told me
that one day you will write books and they would be put into
the Library of Congress.
Many years later, I did not write books, but I am in the
Library of Congress–for patents.

PREFACE

The document that follows are stories about my life, my thoughts and ideas. The ideas I have include ways to approach the problems we have had for too many years. The first thing I would tell you is that I am not a writer. It is not what I do or enjoy. What I'm doing is simply attempting to portray who I am from my early years to my retirement. My accomplishments and failures. When you read this information you will see my abstract style of thinking. I tend to jump about and my sentences are sometimes written in fragments. (This is more evident in my original manuscript for this document.) A friend of mine who read my work said that at times it is hard to follow. She said that I am writing a "stream of consciousness." (The editor who typed this document has made changes to place my "stream" into a more complete sentence structure that the thoughts can be understood more clearly. Ed. note). As I said, I am not a writer, so please bear with me.

The approach I use is to always follow the simple path. Do not wait for science and new technology to overcome what is before us. Never swing the pendulum from left to right in one sweep. It creates so many more problems that will also be added to the list "to do again." Never use that approach. Today you have seen that approach in our national forests. The pendulum has swung too far toward conservation. It has destroyed American's jobs and that is the wrong way to solve the problem.

The idea is to use two parallel roads: on one road the sign says, "To the Future," and the other road is what we are currently on. On this path we do everything we can to support the world, the world means America to me. You must understand that, "trying to save the world is way too overwhelming." Let's start with us, America, and work forward. By doing that we can speed toward the future. And if each country does the same, thus saving the planet becomes a reality.

Does anyone in the U.N. explain: Middle East your oil will soon be gone?; to countries all around the world, the fish in the ocean may soon be gone?; to America that by allowing our national forests to burn, we will destroy the O2 and all the animals that live there?; to us and all the world that our ice shelves are melting away and what that means.

My plans and solutions are all noted and the simple plan is taken. The solutions, remember are not the final end game. However, they buy us time to reach that road to the future intact with minimum or no harm done to anyone. My father told me that life is like playing baseball, in order to play you must "step up to the plate" and take your swings. If you stand there and don't swing, are you still playing the game? What he was telling me was that in life most people will tell you *it won't work, you cannot do that*, etc. These people are the ones who are always complaining about everything, but never "step up to the plate" to play the game.

I am entering the game to solve the problems. This can only be done by me or someone else like me who will become the President of the United States. Is there someone who sees that what I have written is viable, who would like to do this for the people of the United States?

If a new political party is formed, I would like it to be called, the American Party.

These are the keynotes (synopsis) of what I am saying:

- ✔ Farmers, ranching and farmland—some new ideas on energy and water
- ✔ Changing to ethyl alcohol (C_2H_5 OH) for our fuel use–using farms to produce crops
- ✔ New homes with solar electrical power generation that can be sold back to the grid
- ✔ New homes to be designed and built toward zero energy efficiency goals

✔ Re-use and reclaim our grey water to be used for our irrigation purposes

✔ Establish a pipeline for water from east to ease Midwest water shortages

✔ Forests and our forest personel–swing the pendulum back toward center

✔ Restriction of territorial(?) waters–for protections of fishing industry and ocean life

✔ Re-establish superior teaching methods

✔ Reduce government across the board

✔ Bring all of our military home

✔ Honor the veterans who have been forgotten–Korea and Vietnam

✔ Place a moratoriam on immigration for four years. Deport illegals.

✔ Foreign students who graduate from our colleges, after graduation must return home

✔ Our military colleges should not have foreign students

✔ Income tax laws changed to a fixed percent per level of income.

July 4, 1776

Our Declaration of Independence was signed

A PORTION OF THE DECLARATION OF INDEPENDENCE:

"Prudence, indeed, will dictate that governments long established should not be changed for light and transient causes; and accordingly all experience hath shown that mankind are more disposed to suffer, while evils are sufferable, than to right themselves by abolishing the forms to which they are accustomed. But when a long train of abuses and usurpations, pursuing invariably the same object evinces a design to reduce them under absolute despotism, it is their right, it is their duty, to throw off such

government, and to provide new guards for their future security."

Signed by 55 great Americans

March, 4, 1789

Our Constitution of the United States became the Supreme Law of the Nation. This date may be the most important in our nation's history.

Glimpse of My Early Childhood

Due to the character of my early childhood, I have no political party. No love of devotion to any one religion–but to all religions. I guess I would call myself "a man of the world" who was blessed by being born in America. I am an independent thinker and that started when I was very, very young.

My parents, Grandparents, plus my ten additional grandparents, whom I "adopted" at the age of six or seven, were the key to my upbringing. My Grandfather, Mailho taught me the history of America. My Grandfather, Moses, and three other grandfathers taught me the history of the world.

There was a fish market/restaurant called Spangler's not to far from my Grandpa Mailho's grocery store. It is still there today. Fishermen would bring their catch to Spangler's docks. Grandfather Silva would tell me the fish are here and I would go to the store and Grandpa Mailho would give me about three or four bottles of Coca Cola, Orange Soda and Root Beer. I would put those in my wagon with the side boards and lots of burlap. Off I would go to the dry ice plant west of the store. There, some men would give me dry ice for the soda. Off I went to Spangler's where my Grandfather Silva would be. He would unload the dry ice wrapped in the burlap. Then he placed all types of fish on the burlap in the bottom of my wagon. Off I would go again, up and down the blocks, knocking on doors and delivering the fresh fish. There was one family whose name many of you will know–Billy Martin. The Martin family lived not far from the store. We grew up together and played baseball in Kenny Park near the store. After I gave all the fish away I could return home and eat. My Grandfather would give me 20¢ extra for my work. He would say about saving money, "If you put money in banks they give you interest." I didn't know what "interest" was at the time, but every day I would look at the paper in the store with my name on it and I saw that the 20¢ went up one penny each day.

I kept working and learning history and geography. About 4 months later I noticed the amount I had saved was $5.00! I ran to my Grandfather and told him I was rich. He said, "yes, you are. In fact you may be the richest boy in the world." I did not understand then why he said that. Many years later before he died, he told my dad to tell me I was the richest boy in the world because I'm an American.

By 1946 all of my Grandfathers and Grandmothers were no longer alive. However, my Grandfather was right. They are all still with me today in the year 2007.

I was truly a fortunate young boy. My teachers were great; they had a real love of teaching. They would use the textbook and then "preach" to get across the material. They insisted that everyone ask questions so we could all join in. But I had more than a formal education ...

My Grandfather Mailho taught me a lot about geography, the history of America and about patriotism. He came to this country when he was young and with nothing, much like most of our immigrants. He would work at any job he found and still save money. He finally bought a small building on 821 Delaware Street in Berkeley, California. He changed it into a grocery store. The original area was called Seaside and later it was brought into the city of Berkeley. The store is still there today, in 2007. The city leases out the location now, but it is an historical site.

After his store closed every night, he would give me lessons about the wonders of America. Every night he would teach me about different locations in America. Then each night after our lesson, he and I would walk down the steps to the store, stand in front of our flag and sing, "God Bless America." Every night he did this until he died.

He told me about our flag and said that it was made by a lady (Betsy Ross) about the time of our Declaration of Independence. He said the flag IS our country, like those written documents. The flag you can carry and people will see who you are. When you see the flag, you know you are home. He also brought out a world map to show me where he came from, the southern part of France. My Grandfather never said good things about other countries. He said that, for him, they did not exist. America is heaven on earth! To this day, I have never talked to anyone who had such a love of this country. When I was young, I would visit people in their homes and ask them, "Where is your flag?" I have five flags where I live, most are for my uncles who were in the war and one is for my Grandfather and me.

Grandfather Silva, my mother's father, taught me the history of Portugal and Spain. He explained how these two countries conquered most of the Caribbean, South America and the islands in the Pacific. He said that this was done with very bad intentions.

Grandfather Moses left Poland in 1938. He went to Sweden and then to America and became an American citizen. He taught me the history of the Jewish people and their struggles throughout history. He told me of a place where three religions consider the ground as the holiest of all places on earth.

Grandfather Mohammed, who was born in Persia (now Iran), would read to me from the Koran, then translate what it said in English—"the pillars of the faith." He told me stories of great caravans that roamed over the ocean of sand. I noticed when Grandfather Mohammed would come to the store, my Grandfather gave him work. He was very good at woodcraft. My Grandfather would pay with food and money, but most of all–lamb. He knew a Basque family in the mountains of west of Yosemite who had large herds of sheep. These mountain men would bring 4 sheep or so to the store and my Grandpa would give the Basque family one or two 25 gallon kegs of red wine. I was sent to inform Grandfather Mohammed to come to the store. He would get in the truck and drive to the Kosher butcher shop. He did not have a phone. Grandfather would call Moses, who worked a tailor shop, and they would go to the butcher shop. There the sheep would be killed in accordance to the Jewish and Islamic faiths.

I remember one sad day in my life when Mr. Mohammed came into the store. The Mrs. was with him. He did not look very good and his clothes were a mess. When he left with a large load of food, I asked Grandfather Mailho what was wrong. He said that he had been cleaning the curbs on the street when a truck struck him and knocked him into the gutter. My Grandfather called Moses to stop at the doctor's home and bring him some supplies. After he hung up the phone, I could see how upset he was. He said the doctor cannot come because he has a baby to deliver. But your Grandfather Moses will bring medical supplies. He will arrive in about thirty minutes. I went home to talk to mom to see if she had any clothing for Mrs. Mohammed or maybe dad has some clothes for them. I asked mom if we could buy them some new underwear because I had "lots of money." "Where do you have your money, Bobby?" my mother asked me. "Grandpa keeps it for me in the bank in the store," I replied. "Bank in the store?" she questioned. "Oh, O.K." So my mom left for the J.C. Penney store on San Pablo Avenue. She came back with two boxes. When I asked her, "How much money?" She said, "It was $8.00 dollars." So I went down to the store and said to my Grandfather, "I need $8.00 to pay back mom." So he went to the register and handed me the $8.00. I then loaded up my wagon and headed off to See Grandpa Mohammed. As I arrived I pulled my wagon up onto the porch. They must have heard the banging of the wagon as the Mrs. silently opened the door as soon as I arrived. Grandpa Mohammed came to the door and I asked to come in, they stepped aside and said nothing. I removed my shoes by the front door and pulled the wagon inside and closed the door. They just stood there and I thought something was wrong. Grandfather Mohammed finally said, "What is this?" "They are gifts from me," I answered. They asked, "Who bought them?" I said, "I did." Then they began to cry. Grandfather said, "We cannot accept them." I then said, "You must because one of the Koran's *pillars of the faith* is charity." Then they got down on their knees, put their arms around me and continued to cry. Grandfather finally took out his handkerchief and wiped his eyes and went out the front door. Five minutes later he returned with my Grandpa Moses. They talked a while and Grandpa Moses said, I will fit the pants to you when you feel better.

I left, telling them that I had to see my Grandpa Godfrey, who was not feeling well. Grandpa Moses said, "How many Grandpas do you have, Bobby?" I said, "Eleven." I just met Grandpa Meiser and his wife. They are teachers. He teaches science and she taught biology. I stopped and gave them fish two days ago. They told me to come by anytime. So I studied science and the book *Grey's Anatomy* with them. The book fascinated me, especially the heart, lungs, arteries and veins–our cardiovascular system.

My Grandfather Meiser went to the hospital and died. Mrs. Meiser was so sad that I told her I would take care of her. "Bobby," she said, "study hard and keep on studying–never stop ever." One week later she was admitted to the hospital. I came home from school (which I hated) and my Grandfather told me that Mrs. Meiser asked for you to visit her. I went with Grandpa to the hospital to visit her. She seemed happy and I told her to come home so we could work on my studies. She said, "Sorry Bobby, it is your turn to study by yourself. My heart is failing so you study to learn how to fix it." Remember to study and find answers to fix things." The doctor then pushed me aside and my Grandfather took my arm and we left. She died July 7th, the day before my birthday. On the drive home I said, "So many of my Grandfathers are dying and I will never see them again." "No that is not true, Bobby," he said. "You see, every person you meet that is good, you will never forget them, because they will always be with you, always at your side standing with you. You will never be alone for the rest of your life. In all the things you do from now on, they will guide you because the person you are now and forever is good. They loved you, Bobby, like you loved them." So like Grandma Meiser said, 'go forth into the world and fix things.' When I got home I went into my room and began the design of an artificial heart. It took me almost one month, but I did it. I was nine years old.

Thinking Outside the Box

At the age of six or seven years old, I came under my Uncle Frank's teaching also. He was a brilliant mechanical master of many fields. I would ask the questions, "why and why not and how and how come?" His answers were my first lesson on how

Bob Mailho

one thinks in solving problems. He told me, "You are born into the world and live in a box. As you grow older," he said, "you find out that the world is not a box, but like a large ball. I can prove to you," he explained, "that the world is round. However, it would be easier for you if I made an example from a simple viewpoint. Look at the moon," he pointed out. If I could get there and take a picture from there of the earth, you would see that the earth is round. Now what did I exactly do?" he asked. "You went to the moon and took a picture," I replied. "Exactly," he said. "I stepped off the earth (the problem) and took a look at the problem from outside. So when you have a problem, step away to see the problem. Abstract thinking, Bobby," he explained.

So for the next six months, my Uncle Frank would set up problems for me to solve. "Now Bobby, look first at what the problem is, then go away and do whatever you want to, help Grandpa or play baseball, anything. Your mind will look at the problem all this time, because the process of thinking is in another part of your brain."

My Uncle Frank was right. Since that time, I have always viewed problems from "outside the box." Everything becomes clearer and more simple to solve.

My Life as a Teenager through my working years

In my early pre-teens I helped my dad, evenings and weekends, build my mother's first home. It was a major learning job for me. The home was built in Lafayette, California, in an area known as Lafayette Oaks. The home had lots of brickwork and huge bay windows. I think the property was about 1/2 to 3/4 of an acre. After about three years, I asked my dad if would we could have a swimming pool. He said OK, but I was to complete all the drawings, for drainage, power, elevations, type of pump used and locations, material, rebar spacing and size, etc. Then I would dig out the pool area to size for gunite application.

I completed all the drawings, although a few had to be redone for errors. I located all my school mates and said, "We are going to build a swimming pool, so come over on Saturday to help dig." We had two wheelbarrows and many shovels, picks, and rakes. We worked until noon, when my mom fixed lunch for everyone, then we went to work again. At about 2:00 pm the group started leaving. By 3:00 pm, everyone was gone. I worked until dinner time.

The next day, Sunday, I was on my own. About five or six months later the pool space was shaped to size and winter set in. During the winter I had to continually fill in areas due to soil erosion from the rain. The pool was an oval 20' by 40'. Then my mom and dad sold the home and we moved to Alamo, California. We never finished the pool and I was devastated. However, I recalled my grandfather's words of many years ago; "You may work for a goal and never achieve it, but go on and go forward, one day you will have your goal."(He was correct. Today, (2007) I have a 20' x 40' rectangular shaped pool.

In Alamo, we rented a home while my dad built us another home. I believe I was about 14 or 15 years old at the time. The property backed up to a large creek and across the creek were beautiful orchards. This property was owned by a wonderful family, Mr. & Mrs. Engelhart, who were "the best" and I loved them both. They were so good. I worked on their ranch, which I believe, was about 2000 acres. This ranch had almost all types of livestock. The creek between our property and the Engelhart's property was quite wide, maybe 20', and it was deep, with lots of boulders. A horse would not like to get into that. It would be so much easier to get to work if I could walk to the Engelhart's property, but the creek presented a problem. So I told my dad I was going to build a bridge. I went to the library—my second home—and brought back books on all types of bridge constructions and found the type of bridge I needed. I built the bridge and anchored it on my parents' property. On the Engelhart's property I allowed it to slide, to compensate for weight and expansion. It was about 24' long by 4' wide. We were able to bring horses across. I sometimes wonder if my bridge is still standing.

Working on the ranches as a young man, I came to my first real understanding about our environment, which includes all things. Working with animals, caring for and feeding them, taking care of their medical needs, making sure they had clean water, and that their homes, the stalls and barns, were clean. At one ranch, "The Golden Eagle Ranch," which I believe was in Concord, California, they had a large herd of sheep. We worked this ranch for hay baling and sheep shearing. Another ranch was in the Volcano/Jackson area in the rolling California foothills. On that ranch they had Black Angus cattle. It was hard work, but a great life. These were a great learning experiences, not from a book.

Would it not be great for most all city youngsters to experience the grandeur of living in and around nature at its best, to learn about how our crops are produced by planting, watering, and harvesting? Experience it by doing it themselves.

When school was out in summer I found odd jobs as a carpenter's helper, as a plumber, sheet metal worker, and electrician. I was not sure what I would do when I graduated. I took mechanical drawing in high school and studied a lot about architecture on my own as well as learning a lot from working with my dad. I was fascinated with Frank Lloyd Wright's style and elegance. His structures were never from a mold. Each one spoke a different language and style, adapted to the place and person.

My dad continued to build homes. He was hired to work on a home designed by Frank Lloyd Wright in Orinda, California, for Dr. Buehler (who invented a special bomb site during WWII.) My Dad did the drawing of each home, which would be designed for each family's own personal needs. Later I did all the drawings for my dad. I loved it. To understand that, on your drawing board you were building an idea of family. The home must be a part of that family, in all aspects. A great home is a family member. Later in my life, I designed a home I believe Frank Lloyd Wright would love.

My father told me one day that he was going to have to go to work for someone else. He said, "I am losing money on each home I build." So my parents sold the home and we moved to Cupertino. Cupertino was a farming area, with miles and miles of orchards. I found all kinds of jobs in the area. During late summer I worked in the orchards on the Johnson Ranch picking fruit. There were all kinds of fruit, but apricots were the largest crop. Mariani's Foods, in Cupertino, processed the apricots, mainly into dried fruit. They are still in business today. The Johnson Ranch is gone and homes are there now. How sad!

After I graduated from high school, at 17, I started my own business tuning sports cars. I was soon overwhelmed with work and after a couple years I realized that I could not be as meticulous as was needed for tuning a sports car. I could not do my best for each car. So I told each owner that I could not work on their cars anymore. I gave each of them a complete record of their car and what I did to tune it. I had fallen into the same problem that my dad and my grandfather had, you give too much of yourself to others. That's true, and it's OK, because that is who I am.

One of the men for whom I tuned an XK3.8 sedan each week, worked at Lockheed Missile and Space Division and got me a job there. It was OK, but there were too many people running around not doing anything. After about 2 years I left Lockheed.

I went to Denmark to visit a friend and we were to tour Europe together. I had been there only a few days when my friend decided he wanted to go home. The company for which he worked, Haldor Topsil, hired me to take the job my friend was leaving. Haldor did foundry work for the semiconductor industry. I worked in the crystal growing department, a fascinating art form, and there I learned to grow straight diameter controlled crystals which are used for wafer fabrication. I spent two years in Denmark, then returned to the Silicon Valley and went to work for General Micro Electronics, on San Ysidro Way in Santa Clara.

I worked swing shift and taught the art of growing crystals straight and even with a consistent diameter. I took each person and spent time teaching them individually.

But I soon found they did not need me anymore—those women were the best—so I wandered around the facility looking for something to do. I entered into a drawing room with one man all alone there. He sat at his drawing board and seemed to be very short. I went over and introduced myself. He got up and stooped over. He was a hunchback. He became my mentor in the semiconductor world. Each night I would spend a lot of time with him, talking about machines, boats, etc.

One Friday night and I asked him what he was doing, what were the sketches he was working on. It seemed that this company had taken on a job to develop a new and very large epitaxial (shortened in the industry to epi) reactor. He said, "I have 4 graduates from M.I.T. working on a layout of the design." I asked what were the requirements, size, etc. He said, "We did not get any specifications." I said, "That's a real problem that cannot be solved if you don't know the specification." "Yes," he said, "that is a major problem."

On my way home I began to think what are the maximum sizes in graphite, quartz, etc. Those two items may be the limits of the size of a reactor. Saturday morning, off I went to my drawing board. The more I got into the design, the faster it went.

Sunday I hit the board again. Monday morning I slept in until 10am.

My job started at 3pm, and at midnight the shift was over, I went in to see my mentor, Colin Howen. He was grumbling to a guy about the sketch in front of him. When the engineer left. I said, "I made a few sketches over the weekend. I hope you don't mind." I put them on his drawing board. He said, "You like big paper for sketches." "Yes, I do. I like to work full scale," I replied.

He got up, limped over to the board, and looked down. "These are not sketches. These are drawings." He saw my notes saying do not know about some specific items. "Why are you saying that?" he asked. "Because I don't know," I said. "They seem to be related to electrical power," he noted. "Yes," I said. "I can do that portion," he said. "Do you want to take over the design on the mechanical?"

So he transferred me to his department and let all the other engineers go. After about two years General Micro Electronics was sold to Philco Ford Micro Electronics. The entire company and all of the equipment was shipped to Philco Ford on the east coast. Colin and I finished the machine, test fired it, grew epi, and it was done. A group of military men showed up and Colin fired up the machine. Someone signed off the run. The reactor was boxed and shipped to Wright Patterson.

Colin was going to join Philco on the east coast and wanted me to go, too, but I did not want to go. It was a very sad for me when he left. What he gave me was one of the greatest of all gifts, his knowledge of mechanical components, material science, O rings and their proper relationship to metals and liquids, design tolerances, temperature expansion of different material, chemistry and physics, boats and their designs, and much more. So I was turned loose once again to find new challenges.

And I found a new challenge at Fairchild Semiconductor. Here was a company that built and designed almost all of its equipment in-house. Epi reactors, crystal growers, lapping machines, polishing saws for slicing crystals, X-ray machines. There were called foundry equipment. It is the beginning of device manufacturing and I worked in crystal growing. My first job was to increase machine size to grow larger diameter crystals. They had 44 machines. I increased the size of the machine by increasing the reactor chamber. The power input also had to be enlarged; that part was completed by an electrical engineer. There was an extra machine in the corner with the designation 01. It was the original prototype. I gave it the larger diameter equipment also, but I added a totally new design feature. This machine was capable of automatically growing a crystal's diameter. It had some problems, but they could be worked out. I was called to the front office of Dan Martin. He was the plant manager in charge of the foundry division. He complained of a problem with poor diameter control in crystal growing. I agreed with him and told him, "We are hiring people—women—off the street and only spend a couple of hours teaching them how to grow a crystal. It cannot work that way."

"They have a supervisor on each shift," he responded defensively.

"Yes, they do, but those guys do not know how to grow crystals, either," I said.

So Dan Martin gave me the responsibility of teaching new personnel. I started with swing shift, then moved to graveyard, and finished with day shift. Two and a half weeks later all three shifts were growing great diameter controlled crystals. The looks on those women's faces was priceless. There is a sense of great pride when you know you did an outstanding job. The team of women on swing shift produced 360 inches of usable material. That means, if you cut off the top and bottom of the crystal, what you have left is *usable material*. Minus the material for Ohm's resistance. Graveyard Shift grew 310 inches, and the Day Shift grew 280 inches. Day Shift always takes the hit in loss because of so many distractions. Graveyard's number is less because they work fewer hours. Before the training, swing shift was growing crystals of only about 90 to 120 inches. A little education goes a long way. And that applies to everything we do.

Then disaster struck Fairchild. Dan Martin and Lynn Brewer—chief of the Epi Division—left. A new group of employees arrived and took over the crystal growing area. Some of the women quit and some refused to work. A major meeting was called and I was invited. The question was, "Why are the crystals so bad?" The discussion started on one side of the table and went around. All of the group spoke like they were reading a script. The answer was, no one knew how to grow the crystals! I was the invisible man in the room. The boss looked at me and said, "Do you have anything to add to this discussion?"

"Yes, I do. First of all, I don't know who all these blue suits are, but what the women are saying is, 'These guys grow crystals like we did when we started work!' So I'm not going to blame them, because they were hired by the biggest idiot who runs this group. That's where the problem is!"

The boss at the end of the table, whose face first went pure white, but then quickly turned Ferrari red, got up and left. Everyone else left the room. I went down to my drawing room in the basement. Soon someone came down and told me I was fired and had to leave now.

"What is the reason I'm being fired?" I asked.

He said, "The boss said you did not do anything for Fairchild."

I said, "What about the drawings I created?"

"I was told to destroy all drawings," he told me. So we went to the files and removed all the drawings I had made for all the departments I had worked in. We threw away about 130 pounds of vellums that went into the burn box.

Fairchild was a great company. The people who worked there were the best. Fairchild was the mother of all companies on the west coast. The leaders of almost all new companies in Silicon Valley came out of Fairchild. Unfortunately, Fairchild was going down the drain. Its main problem was the top people. We have seen this in the last few years, Enron, Worldcom, good companies, bad leadership.

I went home and in about 30 minutes Lynn Brewer called from Applied Materials and said "I'll see you here tomorrow at 8:30 am. I have a great project for you."

Applied Materials had a contract to build almost 20 large horizontal epi reactors for Motorola. To save machine costs and material, I turned to one of man's oldest developments—casting. I spent three days at a local foundry in San Jose to learn and understand the art form of making castings. I made most of the parts out of castings. I drew casting drawings. Usually you do not do that, but rather, the foundry pattern maker takes the finished drawings and works from that. I gave them the pattern drawing and the machined finished drawing. The pattern maker would make small changes, radius in the corners, or draft angles. I noted all these and began to truly understand the art form that dates back to the bronze age. The end cap on the front of this machine had the Motorola M symbol cast into the cover. It was a beautiful machine. When the third machine left, I went to Brewer and asked him, "Do you have any more machines?"

"Not at this time," was his answer. "OK, well I guess I'll go then," I said. "Where are you going?" he asked. "I'm going sailing, for maybe two or three years." To learn, to learn—that's my life's cycle.

My mentor, Colin Howen, and boats? Well, I bought a fiberglass hull from a boat manufacturer in the northwest and worked on the boat in the mornings before work for about two years.

It was a beautiful sailboat, 35 feet long. I sailed out and was gone for almost two years. What I learned out there was who I was and where I fit into this world. I was born to design things, that is my destiny, I decided.

I entered the United States at Shelter Island Cove, San Diego. They have visitor docks but you can stay for only so long. I decided to sell my boat and become a landlubber once again. I had noticed that the floating docks were quite old and in bad condition. I made some drawings in my boat about the docks, materials needed, floats, bolts, etc. I handed them to a yacht club member and told him I was selling my boat at Kenenburg Marine Yard next door. I offered to rebuild the docks for dock space for my boat plus $10.00 per day for food. I built a lot of docks for them and then my boat was sold. (While I was working on the docks, I caught a thief who had been stealing lots of equipment around the yacht harbor. The local paper picked up the story, sometime in 1969 or 1970.)

After I arrived at home again in Cupertino, the phone rings. Good ol' Brewer was on the line and says, "Bob, I have a new machine for you. Be here on Monday," and hangs up.

There I was, back at Applied as requested. I saw all the old faces I once left behind. The new machine he shows me is the AMC lamp heated reactor. Very beautiful, small, and everything is machined. I open the lower door to see the workings of the reactor chamber. Copper tubing running everywhere, it's packed, no room for working.

I met the man who designed the machine. I'm now in my thirties and this time and to me he's an old guy. I see his drawings and they are PERFECT. I can see old school techniques here. I asked him, "Why is the reactor frame so small?" He said, "They wouldn't let me increase the footprint." "Yes, I see. So you had to place 10 pounds of shit in a 5 pound bag, as the saying goes." He laughed, "No, 20 pounds," he said. His first name was John. I'm sorry I have forgotten his last name. I do know what he did was superior. A truly great designer.

Working on the job was impossible. Remember, it had 20 pounds in there. To get to any components, one had to dismantle half the machine. What I wanted to do was figure out, way into the future, what would this machine evolve into. So after making layouts of the reactor chamber, I came up with the size requirements for the frame. This frame was also important as it became part of the reaction chamber's cooling loop return. I fabricated all aluminum machined parts—castings once again—rubber hoses were used instead of copper and the hoses were color coded. Big cost saving in materials and labor over the copper version.

A young man named Glenn Pfefferkorn was the design engineer who designed, and also added, some very nice features to the frame. He also redesigned the gas panel. His panel was the best, function was superior, and I said, "Change the color of the gas panel to Gloss Black." (Applied had a policy that gas panels will only be white.) "Oh, gee. I didn't get that memo." Glenn also added a plexiglas window in the gas panels, down where you could see the gauges. A light was also installed. This machine, the AMC 7000, became the flagship of Applied for many years. Glenn took over the manufacturing of this product.

I went back to the drawing board to look toward the future. What came out was the AMC 7600, with five lamp modules instead of four, as on the AMC 7000. It also featured many simple design features to ease manufacturing and material costs. This machine was big in all ways, except the frame. The 7000 frame served this machine perfectly. Its main purpose was the reactor chamber, which, being much larger in diameter could now serve the larger diameter wafers. That's a big deal in fabs.

Then the AMC 7800 was born, with the same size reactor chamber, five lamp modules, plus this machine featured far more computer controlled systems. It could also work under low pressure.

That was the last machine I designed for Applied. I loved my work there, but not the politics, which really started to show its ugly head. I never received any recognition for my inventive work. I was the main factor in bringing these machines to the sunshine. In fact, the original frames "7000, 7600, 7800," were designed for the next generation six lamp modules, enough to run eight inch diameter material. It never happened. Someone at Applied could not look into the future!

I left Applied again and went to work at a wafer fab house called Epitaxy, Inc. They had all kinds of equipment for wafer and crystal use. They took me through their plant and I stopped in at their crystal growers room. Upon entering I stopped dead in my tracks and asked, "Where did you get the crystal growing machines?"

He said, "Siltech builds crystal growers."

I laughed and went over to really examine the machine up close. Yes, there it was. Before me was the Fairchild 01 reactor with auto diameter control. I had heard, years before, that

Fairchild scrapped the 01 machine completely. Thank you, Siltech, for finishing the job.

So I began work at Epitaxy, inc. The main reason Epitaxy, Inc. wanted me was because of the man I had worked with at Applied. He was their top guy to oversee the installation and trouble shooting Applied's machine, Bob Dixon. The owners wanted a barrel reactor like Applied's, but it was to be installed for fab work within Epitaxy, Inc.

So I started work on an Epitaxy barrel reactor. After about a month I knew they could not really want a barrel machine. They liked simple machines, low costs, minimum maintenance, and easy operating features. I went out to the fab area. There were horizontal machines and a bunch of AMV 1200 Applied pancake reactors. I watched the epi technicians loading wafers. Some were 2" in diameter and others were loading 3" diameter wafers. But not many, because of the suscepter size—12 inches. So I knew at that moment, all they really needed was bigger capacity.

After work I went home and designed a larger pancake machine. It was not large for me. I had already done this years ago with Colin Howen. An 18 inch diameter pancake, a "piece of cake." Three nights later the entire reactor chamber was drawn.

I walked into work the next day, I put my salesman's hat on. The two owners were there with Bob Dixon. I proceeded to talk about the benefits and faults of the barrel reactor. I told them,"I believe what you are looking for is a higher capacity machine. You have in your fab area the work horses called AMV 1200. However, they cannot process larger wafers efficiently. So, I propose this as an option." I laid down all my drawings of the 18" pancake and then said, "On page 3 you will see the wafer capacity of different size wafers. I'll leave them here for you to look over. I'm going outside. It's a beautiful day."

After about an hour Bob Dixon came outside for me. I went in and the questions started. The short story was, I got Glenn to come over from Applied Material and the two of us completed the reactor together.

Some time later large groups of Applied people joined us. A new company, Epitaxy Equipment, Inc., was then formed. They moved the operation to a new facility. I stayed at Epitaxy, Inc. and started work on a new crystal growing machine. When it was completed I looked to the future and a new machine was created on my drawing board. The group at Epitaxy equipment had named their reactor Gemini 1. So, on my drawing board, my new reactor became Gemini 2. The owners came to me and asked if I minded if they gave my new drawings to the equipment company. "No, I don't mind. However it might be better to have, say, Glenn, come here. I will go over the drawings with him. You know, transfer of knowledge?"

So the boss went and cornered them. But after two weeks, no Glenn. I told the boss. He said, "Yes, I know. They are very mad because they were not given the chance to input the new machine! Would you go over there and work something out?" Sure, no problem. I went over and showed them the new machine. One guy said it would have been better if you had given us the chance to make changes and inputs. I think he came from Applied. "A new breed!"

I told him, "You see this pencil, paper, and eraser? Make your changes." What I did was send out for all their inputs, in writing, with their signatures and date. I did not want to see any of the standard sales pitches, just the designer's information only.

Two weeks went by and not one paper came back. During that waiting period I kept busy reading Engineering magazines, etc., and I also went into the layout stage—full scale—of the reaction chamber. I drew into the water jackets in the chamber, with a number 3 lead, a picture of me sailing a very small boat with dolphins jumping around the it. The boat was so very small. You had to look very carefully to see it. I was so bored. So then, I began to finish final drawings of the entire chamber. One of the bosses came over with a new guy. He wanted to see the layout of the chamber.

This new man, Roger Cory, was going to make a layout of what I did. The boss said, "I need this right away." Roger said, "It's going to take over a week to do them." The boss got angry.

"Well, I'll take these and I'll bring it back." So he took my original layouts—with me sailing in the water jackets.

Roger and I made a great team. We really worked well together. He wasn't a complainer. His drawings were so accurate. He used a set of calipers for increased accuracy in the layouts. In fact, his layout of my machine drawing set fear in the heart of the engineering boss, who said, "Anyone could find out the exact scale of the machine!" God, such simple minds at work!

The company was afraid of introducing the Gemini 2 to the public just yet. They feared that this machine would slow the sales of the Gemini I. I believe they were right.

Epitaxy Equipment, Inc. was reformed. It became Gemini. I left the company before this happened and went back to Epitaxy, Inc. I worked on the final drawings of the new crystal growing machine. Somewhere, somehow, the Gemini group was bought by Lam Corporation. Lam also absorbed the Tetron Company and the monster machine, the Tetron I. A great machine with some very innovative design features. The only problem that I saw was the use of a secondary heat source—a lamp. Applied won't like that!

I have never understood why Lam Corporation bought the Gemini and Tetron line. They were not really versed in that type of business. Then the economy did its cycle down and sales fell way off. Lam wanted to dump its two latest acquisitions.

I was called by Lam Corp. to work in the epi machine area. It was like old home week. Some good faces still there and some bad.

So a new company was formed, Concept Systems Design (CSD). The old Gemini group and Bob Dixon acquired the Gemini line. Bob Dixon wanted me involved in the new company. My principal job was building replacement parts, totally interchangeable with the standard Gemini reactors. I enjoyed re-doing the machines, mainly to make the Gemini reactors better. Better means that when small problems occur, after many months of operation they can be observed. Once the problem comes up, you can see it and redesign the problem out.

One interesting redesign that was given to me was the high power, high voltage, 200kw transfer switch. We bought this unit from Westinghouse. The problem we had was, we were building larger machines that needed greater power. The Westinghouse unit was good. However it was being run above its maximum thru-put. A new unit had to be built. So, Bob-the-Builder is given the job and loving every minute of it. Here I am, a mechanical man, changing hats to work on high voltage equipment. I then returned thoughts to my past, and Colin Howen, my mentor and friend, when he was working on the transfer switch he designed for my original epi reactor over thirty years ago. I recalled his teaching, how, why, what to use, etc. And it was crystal clear how to design this product. I had an advantage over Colin, due to the advancements of material sciences and chemistry. The transfer switch was built and tested. It worked!

The great advances in the fields of material science and chemistry in the last 40 years are astounding. I suppose most of this technology is due to our advancements in space technology.

I took on the next project, a new and very big epi pancake design reactor. I designed the entire reactor and it was, I believe, the most beautiful epi reactor anywhere. It had many new features not found on any machine of its time. We fired it up in nitrogen and it ran OK. We did not have a place to test it with process gasses, so the Gemini 4 just sat. The normal cycle of business started on the down slide. We were OK, but not great. I took on a completely new concept of reactor. I had drawn it on a napkin at lunch one afternoon. I showed it to our Japanese representative. I designed the chamber, full scale, at home over the weekend. I showed the drawings to our company president. He invited a large group of Ph.D.s and managers in companies within the United States to meetings to discuss this new concept. It took quite a few meetings to present the machine. After it was over, the consensus was that it had possibilities due to its black body chamber. Our representative from Japan spoke to many fabs in Japan about the new machine and they sent over a large group to review the design. Our president brought in a Ph.D. to oversee the completion of the design and to build a prototype. After we got the major chamber parts assembled, the Japanese came back and one company who builds robotic and electronic equipment wanted to fund the project. We built the prototype and tested the concept. We had some problems but they were taken care of.

Then the economy in Japan went downhill. The company that funded the machine pulled out of the project. Concept's sales were dropping off. It was decided to find an investor or company to pick up Concept Systems Design. We found it in a good company called Mattson Technology. This company bought an Epitaxy products line. However, their expertise was in an entirely different equipment line. Remember the saying, "If you do not understand the history of the past," meaning equipment technology, "the future of what you do will fail." And so it did. Just like Fairchild did many years before. So before long Mattson sold the Gemini line back to a new group, again called CSD. But before doing that, Mattson Technology chopped up the Gemini 4 and the new concept, black body design. The only negative thought I had is, "Why do companies destroy machines they no longer want? I asked the Mattson CEO to donate the machines to engineering schools. Their answer was, they didn't want technology to be released to others! I left the company and retired.

The last machine I designed used a very different approach to the use of R. F. induction heating. I required six different areas to run at six different temperatures and six controllers. It sure looked easy on paper, but it was not. The first thing stated was, "It cannot be done." I said, "Look it over again and give it some thought." One month later I got a call saying, "We can do it."

How I love those abstract thinkers! They did it, all right. The company was called Advanced Energy, in Colorado. What this company accomplished is like the thousands of other companies here in the United States. Some people will say, "You can't do that." Someone will hear that and move around them or roll over them. Understand that each person can do amazing things, for yourself, for the company for which you work, but most of all, for the United States of America. Be part of America. Don't sit on the sidelines.

I wrote about the importance of each and every American. The companies I worked for would not be here today if they did not have all of the thousands of people in the United States who produced material and equipment for each and everyone. After a design is completed, it will go from drawings to materials. Now almost all raw materials come from mining—approximately 60%—and that one operation, mining, has been in man's evolution from the beginning.

The machines that I've worked on primarily used <316L> stainless steel within the chamber. The machine shops I used were the best. I had a very good rapport with them. The owners of one company in particular, Alweld Machine and Fabricating, were my mentors in machine tool and welding capabilities. The owner, the late Virgil Owens, was a great man. Virgil was gifted in welding. His partner, Tim Smith, was also very good. His specialty was in the area of machining. In fact, I believe Virgil was certified for submarine welding. They started out in what we would call "a garage operation." They now have three very large buildings. Every company I worked after I left Fairchild, used Alweld for the major components. They always did an outstanding job. The best part was, as they grew, Tim and Virgil would teach each new person they hired the finer points about welding and machining. Here is an example of the absolute success of a company who taught their employees to how to succeed. It built company loyalty.

One problem within our country is that the major players in very large industries do not give enough credit to the thousands of smaller industries that made the big guys what they are today.

A BRIEF OVERVIEW

I have covered about myself, who I am from my early years to now. The purpose was for you to understand me, the process of my life and why I think like I do.

I started this project in about February of 2007. I was in search of answers–"why?" Unfortunately, the more I went forward, the more I seemed to step back with more "whys." Why not and how come? I became overwhelmed with so many problems that each problem would flow into the next. I began to see a pattern; our government cannot solve the problems or they don't care enough to make it happen. It was very hard for me to believe my observation, but the issues before me have not made any meaningful advances! Weak education and tenure, crime prevention, health care, illegals, environmental problems, fuel solutions, forgotten Americans, loss of our middle class, political candidates and the unbelievable personal slandering instead of presentation of solutions to our issues. Political religion a whole new trend of alarming proportions. The attack on our Bill of Rights, government give away programs to foreign nations, lifetime pay for government officials–all these are problems. The depletion of our ocean's fish by all nations of the world, the world's overpopulation explosion, loss of American jobs to overseas or to illegals, mining operations closed, too many forest fires depleting our resources and the purchase of lumber outside the US, the formation of the monopolies in our media which is controlled too much by political leanings, buying raw materials from outside sources when we have those materials within our borders, little progress on our depleting water supply, our overcrowded prisons which release criminals to solve problems, give aways for illegals and no money for our own poor, our weak electrical grid that needs new sources, our slow progress with humanitarian aid to flood victims, governmental controls and subsidies of farming, our judicial system allowing pork bills and riders to prevent passage of needed bills–zero accountability by Congressional leaders (lack of scruples a major problem)–and so many more.

I will stop the list at this point.

After going over so many of these problems, I thought who could I trust to read what I have written and "sign on" so to speak? Who will move forward to implement solutions to these problems for the PEOPLE AND NOT FOR THEIR POLITICAL

PARTY, folks!! So I have looked at each candidate running for President. Unfortunately, I saw only people who are so far entrenched in their political ideas that they have no idea, no plan to solve these problems. Therefore everything stays the same. So my only option was to become a candidate and start a new party–the American Party. The symbol for this party would be simple, the American Flag.

Now why would I prefer the Presidency instead of a House Member or Congressman? It's simple! Those in our legislature do not have the power like that of an Executive Order available to the President. I would prefer to see a number of people take over for me, but I would need to know and speak extensively with them first. Right now I have a group standing with me: Me, Myself and I. But, you see, the idea is there and it's a beginning. I have no money to place into a campaign and don't really know how to start a new party. Perhaps all I have is the "seed level," not even the grass roots, we are not there yet. However, many of you who have read this truly believe that most everything I've written could be begun. I'm sure there must be some of you out there who could step up and become the American Party's President.

We always hear about someone not having the experience to be President. I ask you, who of the candidates running truly has the experience to be President? The answer is, "none." What they do have is political connections, former governors, former President's wife, and people of vast wealth and power. Most of these candidates have been in power of some type forever. That is their experience. These problems I bring up have been around since they have been "in power" and longer. They still have no plan that they are willing to promote. They speak very eloquently, not saying anything specific. So what does that mean? To me it means that they have no clue how to solve any of the problems. Period.

I am not, at this time, explaining other areas in need of review or change. We have so many topics that have been ignored, forgotten or just basically not important to our Congressional leadership to warrant its attention. What I will do is list some areas without going into much detail yet.

1. **Trade Agreements:** These tend to be one-sided due to lobbyists who are paid enormous sums of money to work against the best interests of the American people. This borders on SEDITION.

2. **Our Infrastructure:** Roads, bridges and many public works areas are in need of repair and have been for a long time. Some years ago, the California Assembly came up with a fair way to build and maintain California roads/bridges; it was called use tax (tax revenues for road use only). It worked great for a while. Then a new government was installed in the state capitol with its new followers. They saw other ways to use that money for who knows what all. California is now left with unfinished roads and freeways in serious need of repair.

3. **Prisons:** (Are we still calling them that or do I need to say Penal Institutions to be "politically and socially" correct?) Our prisons are overflowing and we release prisoners to commit crimes again. It's called the "revolving door" policy and lawyers love it!

4. **Laws protect the criminals better than the victims of criminal acts.** Crimes committed do not match the penalties for those crimes. Examples: A person who copies and sells a DVD could get prison time and a $250,000 fine. A person who robs a bank can get a long prison term if convicted. But what about the person who commits a personal home robbery? They can get off with a slap on the wrist. Where is the protection for the homeowner who has been robbed? He seldom gets compensated for the lost property and often his peace of mind. What about the burglar who gets injured and then sues his victim for the injury? Is this just a rumor or is this

really possible? Victims of the crime are the ones getting screwed here under our present "justice system."

Our laws give the criminal protection: "insanity," "under the influence" (of drugs or alcohol), child abuse when growing up. No responsibility for their actions. Basically, they get away with it. Other travesties include, "illegal search and seizure" and the failure to repeat the "miranda" in the proper manner.

Millions are arrested each year for both felony and misdemeanor crimes—too many walk way. Too many of these are illegals.

The Three Strikes Law is a joke. Since 1990 the states and Federal prison population was about 770,000. In 2002 the population jumped to 1,427,000. Why are we housing illegals at our expense!! So ask yourself, is the three-strikes law really doing the job?

Prostitution, via the vice squad, arrests are almost 100,000 a year. Does anyone remember the prohibition laws, or better yet the gambling laws? Both were a poor idea from a legislative standpoint. Both of these types of "moral legislation" laws in most states are now gone. Gambling and liquor are now just a part of our GNP.

The District of Columbia, our great seat of power has a crime rate that is, I believe, the greatest in the nation. This is the home of the Declaration of Independence and the Bill of Rights, home of the lobbyist, the Executive and Judicial Branches of our government. This is embarrassing! How is it that these power groups cannot seem to clean up their own back yard–or house, so to speak? And these are the people who make laws that look after us all–to protect *we the people!*

5. **NAIS –National Animal Identification System**

The implementation of this mega bureaucracy identification system is run by our USDA. It is a program which intends to "bar code," as such, all animals used for human consumption. It is meant to track any diseased animal or out break of disease from that animal and any other animals (or processing) that have contacted this animal. From what I've read, this program began with our mega-farms and ranches.*

These groups worked with the NIAA–National Institute for Animal Agriculture. The bottom line sounds like to me another international program that will be forced upon us. Although I am not sure about the costs, nor implementation of this program, is sounds real bad to me. Any time I hear about ANY program that affects our food supply/production, I would be prone to stop it by Executive Order if needed.

The NAIS program has cost you and me almost $100,000 to design and implement so far* and this is just a "drop in a lake." It's purpose is to keep the food supply safe? So please stop telling me that we do not have the funds for the projects I've proposed.

6. A better form of accountability is badly needed within our government.

INTRODUCTION

Approaching the problems we have in America is similar to designing a machine. Each individual must inter-relate with each other to make things work. I call that "fit and form." The benefits of what we are designing, I call "function." These three elements are very important to us since mankind began to change the earth from the time of his existence. In the enclosed written material, I will show you the relationship of these problems in today's America and what I'm attempting to do to solve these problems.

My beliefs on many issues

INITIAL STATEMENT: What every great leader needs is great character (a very hard thing to find in Washington D.C.).

• Leaders must have impeccable honesty and ethics, obviously impossible or they would not have needed to form a Committee on Ethics!

• Leaders must be able to stand in front of you and tell how how he/she stands truthfully on any issue. It seldom happens. All answers are gray in context.

SINCE WHEN HAS POLITICS BEEN SENSIBLE, TRUTHFUL, CONSISTENT, OR
SHOWN TO HAVE COMMON SENSE ON ANY ISSUE?

Perhaps being in the political arena, politicians are infected with a virus called access to "too much money and power." No, that's not really it–most came to Washington already infected with that virus.

QUESTION: WHERE DO YOU FIND PEOPLE WITH CHARACTER, HONESTY AND ETHICS?

Well, my Grandfather Mailho understood the truth and I believe him because he was the truest American I have ever known. He asked me who do you know who can stand in front of our flag and with the Declaration of Independence and the Bill of Rights and sing along with "Kate Smith" God Bless America–EVERY NIGHT? He did that with me until he died. That's what I call the greatest American and he was born in France! He told me that there are millions of Americans like me and you and he believed that.

American culture is alive today and I am reaching out to all of you. My duty to my country is to nourish it and bring it back to a country which is "for the people and by the people." We all have a duty and that is to start today to remember to put our country and our people FIRST. Above all nations–the people of the United States will always come first. We will no longer support any other nation. We are the nation above any others. There are no more favored nations, that is not who we are.

I'm writing this paper so you understand what I believe. You may have a different idea of the issues and I will respect you for that. You must understand that our Bill of Rights was not written for any special treatment of anyone. It was written for ALL Americans. That should cover the entire spectrum of the American way of life. No one receives special laws.

ABORTION:

Each individual must make their own decision concerning this topic. It cannot be me or you or anyone, including the court system, telling us what to believe. You see, once you change the wording of the written words of our Bill of Rights, the entire entity of our Declaration of Independence and Bill of Rights will no longer exist. Our legal minds have been trying to change our country to their way of thinking and this is not right. Remember there is no one in our country today who would have been allowed to sign our Declaration of Independence. They do not qualify now or then.

AFFIRMATIVE ACTION:

First of all, I will say that this smacks of racism. When we as a people apply for a college course and the application form asks for "RACE," that is against our Bill of Rights–PERIOD. What difference does the answer to that question make? Well, it adjusts the examiner's viewpoint. When you do that it alters the regulation of grades and aptitude.

What *should* happen is the question? Questionnaires/forms should only ask a person's name, his address and phone number. All other questions on a questionnaire or form will bias or slant an examiner (or boss) toward or against the person requesting admission. All other questions concerning: age discrimination, sex, and perhaps handicap should not be allowed (unless needed for a particular job). I do not like quota systems. If we use a quota system, then why not limit the the number of aides a Congressman or Senator can have on staff? We the people pay them ... what do you think?

MIRANDA ACT:

This is another on of those thousands of laws to protect criminal acts. Let's start reciting the Miranda rights in grammar school–say from the first through the eighth grade. That should cover it. After the eighth grade is a waste of time. By high school many kids quit school and go directly into criminal activities.

NATO:

Within 24 hours of becoming President, I would start the process of seeing all of our troops and families within Europe recalled. Leave the base intact in Brussels, Belgium. We can retain our allegiance with NATO just in an advisory nature–no U.S. military troop employment.

FOREIGN AID:

NO payments to foreign nations. When our troops leave, all debts are cancelled. I believe we have paid way above the price in American blood. We supported all nations during the First and Second World Wars and the Bosnian conflict. We took no land, we occupied no country (as a ruler) and if my memory serves me correctly, we the American citizens never received total payment from the lend-lease contracts. I believe the amount to be in the $25-50 billion dollar range! Americans can no longer forgive debt like it has in the past 50 years.

MIDDLE EAST:

I would like to see our President speak to all the Islamic Presidents in the region. It should be a one on one together at Camp David. I believe Camp David is an honorable location. President Carter was very good bringing peace between Israel and Egypt. President Sadat was the pinnacle of the true Islamic faith. This conference should not be attended by any news media or outside persons–a strictly private meeting.

THE RIGHT TO BEAR ARMS:

I do not own any guns–YET. I see absolutely no reason why people are so upset about people who own guns. All of the gun owners I know keep the guns locked up in gun vaults. Go to the trap shoots or trade shows. No one has been hurt because they own guns. People against gun ownership always say that, "Guns kill people!" I do not understand how people can think this way. Let me change my argument, let's assume a gun says to a person, "Let's go out and kill somebody." So the person agrees, picks up the gun and goes out to shoot someone. So I see it as this, the gun actually kills and the person is the accomplice. Just think, our prison system can now handle (imprison) millions of guns due to their small size. The accomplice can turn "States Evidence" and go free. However, there is a problem. The gun says, "I did not have my rights read to me." So back to court it goes, the new defense attorney (very sharp guys) in his brief states that his client was under the influence of some substance so the jury hears new evidence. The gun owner gave him too much Hoppes oil and he is 18 years old. So the accomplice goes free and the gun goes free because he was underage. The attorney makes his two million per year paid by the people because the gun has no money. GUNS DO NOT KILL PEOPLE—PEOPLE KILL PEOPLE! If you people are really concerned about people dying let's look at cars. Let's take away the cars. After all, cars killed last year over 45,000 people and injured or maimed close to 400,000.

England passed a ban on hand guns law in 1997. However, people are still being killed by bad guys. You cannot remove all the guns already out there. Only the bad guys will continue to own guns illegally, of course. The bad guys have also decided to use knives. The same number of people are still being killed. So England has made a new law making it illegal to carry a knife. Now the same amount of people are being killed with knives. A pocket knife may be OK, but the homemakers are restricted from using butter knives. All meats are now hamburger style. So now the Queen is very upset with her Pheasant hamburger and orders the law not to include her kitchen. (O.K. so I'm joking about the Pheasant hamburger.) All of the Sirs and Lords are upset with gun laws, so they convince the Queen to allow them to have private hunting lodges. So the guns return to jolly old England. I'm serious about the gun laws in England and the knife laws and the "return to royalty" of the gun clubs. Those parts are true.

We in America, probably have over 10,000 laws regarding guns. Has any of these laws changed the outcome of a crime? Absolutely not. The police are tied up in a "catch 22." They cannot enter a known criminal's home or office without "probable cause." How ideal. And when they do go into one these areas and see crime being committed and apprehend the "suspect," cries of racism, use of excessive force, illegal search and so on and on it goes. So crimes continue due to despot criminal attorneys and laws made by Congressional leadership. The laws of our country are worthless unless some hot-shot prosecuting attorney sees a way to advance his career ... perhaps to show his city that he/she will be running for a Senate seat soon. It seems crime does pay!

A town in Texas, I believe it was, was having wave after wave of crime within the town. Homes were being broken into, rapes and assaults, etc. The police force was unable to slow down the crimes, so one brave mayor, I believe, issued a mandate for all of the people within his district. It was mandated that all of the people learn how to use firearms properly, within safety and the laws of self-defense. Notices went up and many of the criminals who may not have been able to read, soon found that guns were being used to stop crime within city limits. Now there's a lesson we, the people, must understand: the police cannot protect us. They are called in AFTER the crime. Use simple math, the number of citizens of your town/city divided by the number of ground troops–i.e. the police force. You will see it is absolutely impossible for any real protections. So the Bill of Rights states the use of firearms as "the right to keep and bear arms." Exactly what our founding fathers great insight meant: citizens protect yourselves. The word "Vigilance" being *a state of watchfulness* in respect to danger to suppress and punish crime primarily when the "process of law" is inadequate. Our founding fathers were the greatest! Webster's definition is pure in understanding.

SOLVING PROBLEMS

Today, as in years past, we have had serious problems. I do not see that anyone of the (political) parties who are always in front of the camera explain how to solve these problems.

However, the game is always to blame. Usually the President, our Presidents, are rotated usually every 8 years and the blame continues again. The only common denominator left is the remaining group–the Legislature. You see, these people have been in office since they climbed out of the crib. So if I was to blame someone for our screwed up laws, the application of laws, as in the tax laws, which are so screwed up no one can fill out their own tax papers. (Including those who wrote them.) I'll bet they pay a (tax) law firm to fill out their forms or 50th floor C.P.A.s. I could be wrong about the tax issue. However, they seem to apply many slippery "perks" for themselves. You know they may have voted themselves in secret, a tax free for life and 200 years into the future. I see no one with character in this group of Presidential hopefuls!

The President must, at all times, have character and integrity.

I have character, and most of all I would tell you how and when these problems will be solved. Not a bland statement which never ever includes our problems. Oh no, no politician will "stick his neck out" and make a hard fast commitment. Never ever!

POLITICS AND ABSOLUTE CORRUPTION:

If I was unemployed and went to the Unemployment Office and they told me there were two job openings: "the first is a Politician." I would say, "I'll take the second choice." "But I did not tell you what the second choice was," they would respond. "O.K., Tell me what it is." "You wrote on the questionnaire about your work talents that you could play the piano. Is that right?" "Yes, that's true," I'd say. "O.K., the second choice is playing the piano in a whore house!" "I'll take it," I'd say. But why, do you ask? Because playing the piano in a bordello is not only honest work, but far more honorable!

Remember when politicians assuaged their conscience with glorious words like, "It's all for the greater good" and "Harm is minimal for all of us?" And "I'm not supposed to tell you this, but ... I get special interest kickbacks from Lobbyists from around the world." "There are from 50-70 thousand lobbyists in the D.C. area. Always remember that one of the definitions of "politic" is rafty, unscrupulous—really!. Oh, I suppose you did know that. Do you or did you believe your Party that you have been so loyal to all your life, really cares about you? Really? I've found out most of those wonderful people who vote for their party have locked onto the idea that Republican Party are money people and they are for "big business" only. They do not care for the working class. The Democratic Party is for the workers, the poor, the unions and give vast amounts of money to causes. Well, they both do that. I've told people that both parties are so similar that you cannot truly see the difference. It cannot happen. Whether you are a Republican or Democratic owner of a small or large factory that person needs workers. They don't care what party you belong to, they only require your qualifications for the job.

Why are so many jobs being given to foreign nationals? Because of another of the failures in our country: to educate our people. It has nothing to do with money. Money is not the "saving grace" of our poorly managed educational system. A new Zealand teacher told one of my closest friends, "There are no poor students–just poor administrators!" Politics, I believe, has destroyed the heart and soul of our teaching profession. How do we change and bring back this greatest of professions? I would say that each of the towns/cities should come under it's own control. Separate it from the state and federal control. Good teachers do not need to be under the control of the millions of political administrators who do not teach. However, they do get paid and the students become lost in the money game. If students become real problems for the teacher, those students must be removed. I was because I kept asking, "Why?" and "Why not?" Any student who creates problems only infects the rest of the class like a virus. So what we have is that no one learns. That's about what we have in the larger cities today. Students are moved from grade to grade not learning anything: can't read, math is gone, English is impossible to understand, but the school gets its head count and pay (from the government). So they graduate. I don't know the graduating level, but they leave and go to work—in petty crime at first and then move on up to major crimes, prostitution, drugs and gangs. We the people of the U.S.A. just lost again, another generation.

I am recommending a real change starting with the Secretary of Education. However, I cannot do anything without your help. The power of the President is quite vast. My Grandfather told me that, "Those who are most suited to power are those who have never sought it." That's me. Just let me spend a few months at that post to do many things and then I'll leave to enjoy the remainder of my life.

Do you recall when my good buddy was sitting in Air Force One at the LA Airport getting a haircut from a barber who gave haircuts to the movie stars?" The entire airport basically came to a halt. Aircraft were diverted to other fields making relatives drive to another location to pick up passengers. That is truly the highest form of "Don't give a shit' power. Who cares if I upset anyone? The worst part is many loyal coat-hangers thought this funny and cute and "way cool."

GIVE AWAY PROGRAMS—Porks Bills and Grants for everything

The above programs are generally funded by lobbyists by way of bribes. As far as I know, Senators receive vast amounts of money to tack on a lobbyist's "Pork Bill" onto the Senate's bills. I think these are seen in the form of a "Rider." I have no idea as to the total amount of money is exchanged for these bribes. We never hear about these "back room games" until you may hear about it on T.V.

The plan I would like to see implemented on bills sent for passage would be what is done by authors of books, television shows and movies, music scores, etc. That is, every bill and rider would have to list somewhere all the members of congress, house or *whomever* the author(s) of that bill are. They would also have to list any contributors (amount given)/supporters/outside companies made toward the passage of that bill. Full Disclosure it could be called. This disclosure would include support or contributions from other countries/entities also. The bills given for signature currently do not have these people listed, just the Senator supporting that bill, even though it may not have been actually written by him/her.

So it would not take up too much time of their TV "face" time, the information could be run along the bottom of the screen in the scroll so those interested would know who and how much was contributed toward any bill.

I believe that by including all these persons and organizations who authored the bill would be an honorable and ethical thing to do. My feelings are that if this information is not willingly given, the Senator comes under the heading of "low life" and is in possible danger of plagiarism of someone else's work!

POLITICS AND THE MEDIA:

Today, and in the past, our political front seems to always look at what today's news media is saying or writing. For them that is the only news worth mentioning. I believe we pay our elected representatives to "lead." At least I was told that was why they are elected. But somehow we have been (again) led astray. So we now pay people to "follow." Just great!

Speaking of the new media, that includes the "boob tube." Our "Bill of Rights" as interpreted by the news groups, allows them to print or broadcast anything they want. The news media are doing a grave injustice to the people. They can use sources whom they protect and these sources can lie to us and on many occasions are still protected. Why?

Now, if I look at the greatness of our framers of the Constitution and see what they set down in print. Did they intend absolutely that "freedom of the press" should include lying, deception, protecting criminal intent, and hiding those who commit sedition? I don't think so. They certainly did not consider the news to be run by politics or political parties, or for one news corporation to own and control what is printed. Why was Ma Bell broken down into small fragments of communication? Someone said, "monopoly." Is that word still used or are we now calling it something else?

SPECIAL INTERESTS/LOBBYISTS:

I am absolutely against ANY form of "special interest" for any reason, because it establishes the basis that a group is of more value than the rest of the people. All of our "Pork" programs are forms of payoff to contributors of a candidate within their jurisdiction. A form of bribes–no it IS bribery. The candidate cannot be elected wihout funds from lawless supporters or at the very least, supporters that see only one side of an issue. You see, the Senator will bribe another Senator saying, "if you vote for my bill, I will vote for yours." These tacked on "Pork Bills" would never pass if they stood alone. They can only be advanced with the use of this type of bribery. Our Declaration of Independence has no room for special interests. Each bill must be able to stand alone.

Lobbyist: to lobby a Legislative House is to transact business with legislators to influence proceeding their personal agenda or agency. Those agencies can be foreign or domestic. The domestic lobbyist means someone within our country wants a law for themselves–to get ahead of others. The lobbyist will use enormous funds to influence that legislator's position. The foreign lobbyist is usually an American who works for a foreign nation. To influence the legislators is the highest form of despotism. How can any American want to allow a foreign nation to affect our laws, to place our families in jeopardy?

I believe that George Washington and Thomas Jefferson would want to erect a gallows in front of the Washington Monument to show the nations of world that the United States of America belongs to OUR PEOPLE and we will not allow any other nation to interfere.

THE MISPRISON OF RELIGION

For almost the last 20 years, I have seen the grave mistake in how religion in our country is taking on what the words state in the Book and how men and women of the pulpit have been preaching to their flock. It appears to me today, that church leaders seem to want to return to our past–a time frame about 1,500 A.D. The rule of how the church was run by Popes and priests. That rule was called money and power. During that time frame of Martin Luther in 1,517, he wanted to reform the Christian church because he did not like the way the church leadership lived their lives. He felt that these men who proclaimed to follow Christ's life lived their lives by setting a bad example: great wealth and great power. He established the protestant revival, meaning "protesting" the ways the church had gone wrong. His example was considered blasphemy with his 95 Theses (errors of the church teachings). Catholics across Europe turned against and executed thousands (France). Spain set up the Inquisition and people of the reformed Christian faith were burned at the stake with a priest holding the cross of Christ in front of them!

Today's leaders do not go around killing people because of their faith, however they found a new way–it's called *political power*. On the news someone from the Bible Belt* told a newswomen their view on the upcoming Presidential election. The church leaders said that we will vote, meaning all of their members, for President the candidate who follows our church's beliefs. So that means that we have gone from killing masses of people to threatening a candidate for President. The candidate's religious beliefs do not mean that he will make a good President. It makes about as much sense as selecting him based on what area of the country he lives in or his social status from which he came. Why? Political power and maybe wealth. We are mixing politics and religion again as back in the year AD 1500.

Have we forgotten who we are, where we came from and why our religious freedom is on the top of the Bill of Rights? Those men came from where it was dictated how you worship and who the leaders of the country were by how they worshiped.

How you worship, when and to whom is what your religion is. It should make no difference what a person's religion or his or her beliefs are. Our forefathers knew all about religious persecution or in the case today, religious discrimination.

To church leaders in the U.S.A., go to your place of worship and speak to your flock about the true faith of Christ: His goodness, love of his followers for all faiths and religions. Teach your followers to extend their hand out not with a sword (or a bomb), but reach out with friendship (the story of Zacheus) to all faiths and nations of this world. Only then will we, as a nation, be following in His footsteps.

ILLEGALS WITHIN OUR COUNTRY:

President Bush is absolutely wrong in attempting to coat over this problem of American law. You never allow criminal behavior to pass through our gates of law freely. NEVER, for whatever reason. Once that door is cracked open, all hope for the American culture is gone. People, we are in a war now and have been for a long time. The Mexican rulers believe that the land to the north belongs to them!

NAFTA was formed and, I believe, it was supposed to help South American nations with a free trade tax arrangement. It's really working great, isn't it? However, I did not know free trade included Mexican nationals and all the other nations south of our border, including criminal gangs and terrorists. These can easily enter our country. I would be the last person to ever say that I am against immigration. How can I say that? We are a country that was formed by immigrants. In fact the only modern nation in the world.

Consider this, if you don't produce a product, distribute, handle it, etc. there is no cost to you. You become what we have in our country who are called the "middle men." So you must ask yourself, why do you think the past Mexican President Vicenti Fox just loved us? (probably similar ideas from the new Presidente Felipe Calderon). He could raise the price of oil he sells to us. He does not have to set up jobs, hospitals, schools, homes, utilities, sanitation facilities, or roads. No, he does not have to spend one peso; "no, no let the stupid gringos take care of the Mexican people". The news media just loves it.

Just recently a woman, an illegal, was going to be deported by Homeland Security. She gave newscasts from a church and demanded that the U.S.A. allow her to stay here. She was planing to go to Washington to tell the President. You know what we should do with her? It's something we did in the Middle East years ago. Let's promote her into power in Mexico and perhaps Mexico just might become part of the (modern) world, not the third world. Would that not be great? We would see a Mexican leader who truly wants to support her people. We could offer her our Declaration of Independence, and Bill of Rights translated into Spanish. Well, maybe we should skip giving them our "Liberty" section or they will still be crossing our borders in droves. Damn, Bob, you do come up with a few good ideas.

Because I can see items in abstract, I can say Mexico will become in the year 2040, the second Democratic Nation, following our Declaration of Independence (that is, independence from us, I hope!). Mexican workers come here, for clean water, jobs, and more $$ than they could make in Mexico. Unfortunately, Mexico has based their government on that of Spain after being conquered by the Spanish. Spain's doctrine was to conquer. Spain has no such document for freedom. Loot the conquered nation and enslave its people was their government's pattern and Mexico still has those same ideas present in their government today.

I have often wondered about the great state of Texas. I believe they wrote into their entry into the Union a clause in which they could become a separate nation. My God, can you imagine what they might do to prevent illegals entering their country? The South will rise again (not only the Texans, but every southern state). At the Alamo, Texans were not the only ones who died to protect their culture. The Texans I've worked with would probably declare war against Mexico and rightly so.

I believe the President should declare this problem a National Security Threat. All llegals in our country should be rounded up (with human care and dignity). They should be processed by finger prints, photographs and name. This paperwork should be sent to the State Department who will submit it to the Mexican Consulate. Here are the options we are giving the Mexican government ...

OPTION ONE:

Recall your Mexican people–use satellite, radio, papers, loose forums at the border crossings. Within this option, the government of Mexico is responsible to it's citizens for their care. Set up jobs, bring clean water, proper sanitation to the forgotten people who live outside the city walls. (Within the city–"the streets are paved with gold" for tourism). Set up schools, medical care centers, etc. Just take care of all the great people of Mexico. That is your job. It is not for the American citizen to support your citizens. If any of these people, on whom we have illegal status records, return to the US the cost to the Mexican government will be $25,000. If one of these Mexican nationals commits a crime in the U.S.A. we will return them to Mexico at a fee charge of $100,000.

OPTION TWO:

Our government should consider Mexico to be a real threat to our National Security. We should do what President Reagan did. Declare an embargo–all tourism from America to Mexico will cease. Border crossings will be armed with military personnel. I do not believe that we would go to option two because tourism is the main staple of Mexico. Besides they could easily set up their nation like Franklin Delano Roosevelt did during our depression. In fact we should look at that same thing to get our people back into the work force. It certainly cannot hurt. (During the Depression F.D.R. set up the Conservation Corp, I believe. They moved people from New York to Oregon, where they were given jobs, food shelter, education. Schools were set up to teach them different jobs. These jobs were the backbone of the Depression recovery. By shipping people out of NY, etc. and moved to a different location, they had to stay–as it was a long walk back home).

I remember on May 5, 2007, I was in San Jose, California. There were cars and trucks running up and down the streets in east San Jose waving Mexican flags–some as large as four to six feet in length. We stopped for gas at a corner gas station and observed one pickup truck with at least six flags in the back pull up to get gas. I got out of my friend's car and walked over to ask what the celebration was about (I already knew). A young man got out of the back of the truck and said, "It was Independence Day." I said, "No," I said, " that's a few months away." "No, no," he said, "Mexico's Independence Day." "Oh," I said, "but this is America!" "Sí, you are right, but in America we are given a chance for so many opportunities that we cannot get in Mexico." That statement said it all.

My grandfather's words came back to me—his words of 60 years ago: "America is heaven on earth." The Mexican people love their country, but their country does not love them back. That last sentence has also become true within our country. For a very long time we Americans have been forgotten. We do not count except for a vote. We cannot sit at a Presidential hopeful's fund-raising dinner because it costs $2,000 to $8,000 per plate. The majority of us do not belong to that exclusive club–that takes money and fame.

IMMIGRATION and POPULATION INFRASTRUCTURE

Our country has always been "Welcome to America." Ellis Island and the Statue of Liberty welcome all to the U.S. For the first time, I would like to place moratorium on immigration into our country for 4 years. This will allow us time to truly look at the total population, not just throwing numbers around. We need to examine our infrastructure, all of our Public Works areas. Are they adequate? Where are the weaknesses? How can we fix these areas and what are the costs?

Today, we do not even know what the total number of illegals numbers we have in this country. The worst part is, as I see it, at our present rate of growth, we will be over 500 million in only 57* years. That's a half a billion, folks. Now that is really a very scary thought. You will begin to understand why I am so strong on the absolute protections for our agricultural land, recycling, our water, lowering our energy usage across the board, changing our fuel to ethanol (to reduce global warming) until technology finds an even better solution, keep our fishing industry sustainable–globally.

Remember also as population grows so do crime issues sky rocket. With the court systems as backed up, the police as under-manned, and the prision populations as over-crowded as they are today what happens in the future with even more crime?

Water issues, already a problem today, will be multiplied. What will we expect–water rationing? People with wells on restricted supply, or forced to go to metered city water systems?

We are a nation of liberty and freedoms. Will our property rights be defended with firearms–by Americans holding their ground? I would be standing with them for our rights to bear arms, because of the Bill of Rights.

---

* Using current US poplulation as: 301,139,947 x 1.00894% to the 57th power. Yearly growth rate .0894%

Our education system cannot seem to educate our young at the population level today. What about at a half a billion people? How many more children must we educate then? How many of them will not speak English as their language? I know for a fact that our present educational system will not expand to include an increase in children. If you look to the past you will see that our educational system did not move ahead during our technology explosion. Our children (all children are mine too) will slip further down the ladder to a third world level where there is little true literacy. We will then become a nation that has lost almost all of our middle income people and what is left is like many other nations–the rich and the poor. This could be caused by our cultural changes we are seeing today.

I believe that it is **mandantory that all children speak English**. Why? Because, if I recall, our Declaration of Independence is written in English, only English. The American flag bows to no nation or king. We will NOT force our children to speak any language except English in grammar school. When they graduate to high school, they have all types of language options for students. They can, if they wish, take classes in any language that is offered. By forcing a different language on them during grammar school, what we have done is take away their right as Americans to speak and write in English adequately–the heritage to which they were born. English speaking parents should tell their schools that they will remove their child from any grammar school class that is Spanish-speaking. Those classes should be used to teach Spanish-speaking immigrants English and *only* for teaching English. To parents who speak only Spanish, your child must adapt to speaking only English at school and elsewhere. If you are here in the U.S.A., speak only Spanish currently, and want to become a U.S. citizen I would recommend you take night classes to learn English. In fact, the truth is, we need to adopt English as our national language–formally.

My grandfather, who came to this country many years ago, spoke only French. He learned English on his own. He told me to become an American citizen you "must speak the language of the land."

Consider this, many nations in the world (including ours originally) have restrictive immigration laws. Some limit their immigration on age and ability, basing it upon whether you will be an asset or a (financial) liability. Well, that eliminates me, I am retired and no longer work. But I have a lot of work left in me. Bob the builder is still alive and well.

People enter our country for many reasons.

- The quality of our life compared to where they came from
- Our unbelievable freedoms (compared to theirs)
- Our bounty and variety of foods
- Our educational freedoms
- Our religious freedoms
- The ability to make more money and live a better life with more opportunities than where they came from.
- Our higher education opportunities

ENTITLEMENTS:

Monetary benefits to many citizens must be looked at again. We cannot have people who have been on the roll call for 20 years or more and not working. America was not set up to furnish anyone a forever wage to do nothing. The major branches of government, Executive and Justice branches, I just found out recently, voted themselves *lifetime pay with full medical and other lifetime benefits*. Now I ask you, fellow Americans, why you did not get a benefit package like that from your employer? Oh, and by the way, what happened to "checks and balances" built into our government? So I get it, our Representative uses the checks and balances between themselves. If my memory is correct, we the people of the United States empower these branches to work for us. Something happened people, now we work for them! Just like the kings and queens we fought a war to rid ourselves of. Now, we have to declare a war on 515 within the legislature. We, the people will decide their wages, perks and benefits and their term in office. Four years sounds good to me, if it's O.K. for the President. I figured a wage of $200,000 per year, plus perks in food, lodging, commercial travel–another $50,000. That amount is way above the upper middle class. So all these years, you people who voted "red" or "blue", never changing your party because you thought your party good and it was faithful to you–looking out for your benefit. Yes, they were, except you see, their game was/is played by "house rules." All entitlements, money, programs, etc. passed through them first and left you NOTHING. Ever wondered why there is no health-care. It's been discussed by four changes of our Representatives. Crime is getting out of control and drugs running amuck, well, they *may* not have entered the kindergarten group yet. Grants are given to schools to study anything and everything. No jobs available in manufacturing as they're sent outside our borders. Aid given to foreign nations comes first. Drunk driving is not a crime and prisons are nearly a three star hotel, complete with medical care. Prison libraries have more law books than the local library. Multiple languages are required in our schools. The list goes on and on.

So all you Americans out there, what are you bitching about? You and I are responsible for this happening. I'm sorry, because the problems we face today are there because we were asleep. Just like Europe after the First World War. They fell for the elegant words of President Wilson in the League of Nations. Everyone is friends, we can go about our lives in harmony. After all, that great statesman proclaimed, "that was the war to end all wars." We, meaning all of us, were asleep because we are unable to cut the umbiblical cord to our party. In fact most Americans are married to their political beliefs even over their marriage to their spouse. Your spouse is a warm, living person and your political party is like a false, uncaring, cold god.

So, are you going to vote for a person who's looks fair and their hair looks good? Or the person who dresses well, smiles all the time even when he or she is lying, but you refuse to admit it. Perhaps that person always speaks what you want to hear, repeats and repeats the same statement even though what is stated does not really say anything you have not heard before a thousand times? Politicians know that if they keep repeating these statements, which have always worked because the political playbook says you will succeed and win by using them. Why do they work? Because those illiterates out there are basically brain dead. You know they are right–we are because we keep going back to them in hopes (what hope?) that they will change something. Sorry they will never do that. Major fund-raising comes from big sponsors who expect something in return. So if you like our system as it stands now, just like it has been for the past 30 years, just do exactly as you always have, but please stop the bitching.

AMERICANS WHO HAVE LOST THEIR HOMES

Recently, I was sitting at my large drawing board, looking over some of my house plans of varying sizes of homes and I thought, we have in our country today thousands of people with no homes. Mostly I was thinking of those that were lost during the hurricanes and flooding along the banks of the Mississippi River.

What I don't know is, how many of these homes have been rebuilt? How many will not be rebuilt, because the people were too poor to afford Homeowner's Insurance? For these lower Middle Class or very poor, we must do something.

The home designs I have been thinking about should

Linda and I gave Habitat large amounts of home building materials. The home I live in now (Sonora, California) has lots of clear heart redwood. This wood was one of Frank Lloyd Wright's favorite woods. Unfortunately, redwood is almost unavailable these days as our supplies of these slow-growing trees dwindle.

While my Dad worked on one of Wright's Home Designs, I spent time looking at this beautiful concept of Habitat. Wright came in and saw me watching my Dad putting this redwood on the ceiling in a rectangular shaped pattern. I said to him that I thought the ceiling was absolutely beautiful. He said, "Did you know that Redwood is like a woman's skin? Handle it gently or it will bruise!"

be viewed as "Pre-fab" modular homes of two bedroom or three bedrooms. Four modules as follows: a kitchen and dining room module; a living room, entry and porch module; two bedrooms with bath & laundry module (including the furnace, water heater). The foundation needs to be placed on concrete posts. Auger down to base rock and rebar. Posts need to be two feet high or higher in flood zones. We would use only standard appliances, cabinets, fixtures and shower/tub unit. Roof configuration—all engineered trusses with hip/gable combinations. No mobile home or trailer components used. Must be efficient to operate in the 80 range on the efficiency (Zero Energy Building) scale.

I would like to see Jimmy Carter and his JCWP (Jimmy Carter Work Project) take up this housing project and continue in that disaster-prone area. He is affiliated with Habitat For Humanity, a great organization, which is the real heart of America. It's culture, spirit and heart, beating for all Americans. In short, it's what America is all about—"for the people and by the people."

Anyway this new project could actually be called *By the People, For the People*. The By the People group is quite large and they are responsible for prefabricating the homes, the delivery of the home to the site, and its hook up to utilities, and the final checks. A Declaration Certificate would accompany every completed home. It would have the signatures of the people involved in the prefab (one page); and the setup/hookup/final check of the home (second page). These two certificates could be framed together and presented to the new home owner in a *For the People Ceremony*. Building homes, like stated above is being done by Habitat groups throughout America. But what I'm talking about is, stepping up mass production in a factory environment. We currently build cars at the 50 to 60 cars per hour in factories. We built ships in 1941 at the rate of 20 per month. I know we could build these homes in an assembly line and they would be great homes too.

O.K. where do we get the money? My question is, how much money do we continue to give away in foreign aid? Now I ask myself, why is it easier for the U.S. to approve financial aid to outsiders (non-Americans) than to Americans? Then the government tells us that we have no funding for America's home use. (see closure of foreign bases)

I would like to see us slow down or even stop foreign financial aid. I want to see us return to the thinking that America comes first. We, in America have been "bleeding" for a very long time in both financial and trade agreements. Sometimes I've wondered if these gestures of our friendship are truly received and returned. However, I've learned that these alliances are not made because of love, but only in financial interest. We must always remember that.

With our two holidays of Thanksgiving and Christmas, family and friends gathering around tables in our homes, remember those without a home. LETS BUILD THESE HOMES!!

THE FORGOTTEN AMERICANS:

In my travels through life, I returned to visiting and working at a geriatric hospital. I was revisiting my early childhood and my love for all my "grandfathers." At first, visiting a geriatric hospital bothered me, then I felt felt that my grandfathers were sitting next to the patients. I spoke to the patients of many things and asked them many questions. "What did you do in your life?" "Where were you born?" When I asked them about their children their faces would light up. Sometimes they would rock back and forth and then their faces would change to intense concentration ... then to a smile. That said, I have returned and asked them about the "horse and carriage days." I asked them about Model "T"s, and the Wright Brothers. These subjects brought smiles to their faces. Some of the patients were blind or partially deaf, it made absolutely no difference. They would put their arm or hand out reaching for the touch of another human. That's what they need. You, as a fully functioning adult, represent the full side of life. They know they are slipping through the door of death soon. You can see that too. As their faces become serene and peaceful, your voice then cannot be heard—another voice is speaking to them.

Many families have a tough time when it comes to taking care of family members. So they put their parents or grandparents into hospitals or Home Care Centers for the elderly. No fault there nor ever will be. You see, I never spoke to my mother or brother when they died. I never was told they died. My father, as he has gotten older just moved into the senile stage very quickly. He was blind and almost deaf, and could no longer walk. My cousin put him into a home in Hayward. Then he was moved to Kaiser Hospital. That's when I learned about my Dad's problems. I was unable to visit him because I was in bed with the worst flu I have ever had. Five days I stayed home. Then I received a call that my father had died on March 7, 2007. Even though I never got to see him on that date, I spent a lot of time with him on August 13, 2006 when the Oakland A's honored his baseball days at the McAfee Coliseum. I love you, Dad. Thank you for my life. We had great times.

Please everyone, take the time to spend with your parents, or grandparents or go to talk to anyone at one of those elderly homes. Do not allow them to be forgotten. One day you will be one of them.

CHILDREN'S CANCER WARDS:

This topic always rips me apart—children's cancer wards in hospitals. Here is a life before you, that is slipping slowly away. You see parents always attempting to be positive. Even the staff have moments of sadness, doing anything that will bring some form of hope, knowing the final results. I have walked around the different wards looking into their faces. They are all beautiful faces. There are no ugly children! I walked into one ward and went in and when I stopped, in the second bed was a child who looked like me. I went to his bedside, told him my name and then told him that he looked like me when I was nine years old. He said his name was Dwight, just like Dwight D. Eisenhower. I said that Dwight was my middle name. I saw a book he was reading

was about old sailing ships. In the next bed was a child reading about cars (Hot Rod Magazine). Another was interested in
trains. I spent a great deal of time talking with them. I would tell
myself to keep up their dreams, never let them falter. I remembered my dreams at the time. So I left the hospital and stopped
at a large bookstore and bought books that I knew they would
love. I left work early the next day and went to the hospital and
up to the children's ward. I didn't bring the books this time,
instead I brought a copy of the Declaration of Independence.
There were two of the children's parents there. I said, "Do you
know who you are and what you are?" I asked, "This paper I
have here tells you and me and all the 200 million other people
out there who we are. Those people told me to tell you how
important you are to them—because they are Americans, like
you, and they love you. I read the Declaration to them; told them
about our fathers of 200 years ago and why July 4th is important to us. I spoke about the people who signed their names to
the Declaration of Independence. How James Madison set the
duties of our President. I told them that I had some wonderful
books for each of them in my car and would be right back with
them. One little boy asked me, "Will those people love me?" "Yes,
they will," I said. "Why do you ask that?" "Because I am black.
"O.K.," I said, "I will ask them about you and I will be back." As I
walked out into the hospital corridor, one of the fathers was sitting there. I could see that he was crying. He called me over and
said, "Thank you." "No thanks required," I replied. "No, there is,"
he responded.

"I admit that I have never read the Declaration of Independence
and I am grateful." I know that many Americans have never read
it.

I went to my car, picked up the books and went back to the
ward. The children seemed happy and were talking about the
words in the Constitution and how nice it was that all those people who didn't know them, loved them. I went back to the boy
who loved trains and steam engines. I said, "I don't know why
you thought that people won't like you (because of the color of

your skin), but whoever told you that was probably mistaken. People make mistakes all the time.

I asked those people about you and they said 'they love you even more and they can't wait to see the steam engine you will build.' But I would like to know what you would name it. All steam engine designers name their engines." His parents, overcome with emotion, left the room. After that I gave the children each a book and started to leave. The nine year old asked, "Are you coming back?" "Would you like me to," I asked? "Yes," they said. "O.K. how about if I come tomorrow?"

I went back many more times and also visited other wards.

Please spend some time visiting the children in cancer wards and other wards. You will make them happy and their parents will love you for what you do. Remember no gifts are necessary. Your presence is all that's needed to make them happy and keep their dreams always ahead of them. Thank you for doing this. Always remember the children are all ours.

My dream of finding some cure for cancer is way above me. It takes an enormous amount of money for research and incredible devotion of the researchers to man the battlefront against cancer. They now know that there are many forms of cancer, some more treatable than others. But the money is always the stopping point. So hear me out. Let's use the money that major suppliers of beer spend on advertising on T.V., newspapers, etc. During the football Superbowl, as an example, CBS is looking for $2—2.6 million dollars for a 30 second Superbowl advertisement this coming January. What if we asked all the breweries in the US to donate the money (to cancer research) that they would spend for that 30 second spot on national TV? The major stations CBS, NBC and ABC could also donate the air time for this effort. The new commercial should scroll through the names of the breweries and where their home office is. The amount that is given is not shown. The money is an advertisement for their product and is thus tax deductible as a charitable contribution. We have many smaller (micro) breweries whose names would also be seen. That would be something that under normal circumstances would not happen due to the costs. The key element in this crazy program is getting the money for the fight against cancer. Our founding fathers drank beer/ale. That was the drink of that time. What could be more patriotic?

CANCER—FINDING THE CURE

I am very sorry that we have not made greater strides in curing this form of pain and death. I am very sorry for the victims and their families. Yesterday, October 17, 2007, I was shopping at Safeway Grocery Store and I noticed many women in pink T-Shirts. I stopped and asked them why all the pink clothes? They said that October was Breast Cancer Awareness Month! I went on my way and picked up my supplies of food and on my drive home, I kept saying, "no, no NO. I forgot so many items after I talked to that woman because all I could think was 31 days? Why do we have one month, only 31 days to remember breast cancer–or any cancer for that matter? We will not use the time or the month to remember something so important to people's lives. Each day of our lives we can and should do something about it.

Michael J. Fox, a great guy, has made his illness (Parkinson's disease) better known to most of us. Through him, research has advanced in this field. This applies to Liz Taylor and her aids work and to Christopher Reeves and his contribution to the field of paralysis from injuries. My feeling is that it should not be important to have someone famous to tell us about cancer in all its forms. We all need to get behind a program to help eliminate this killer of our children and adults. It will take vast amounts of money that would be spent far better than on some of these "pork bills" and grants.

Research personell who are constantly trying to find success in defeating cancer are a tough group. Thank God these people have the stamina and perseverance to continue year after year in search of breakthroughs in treating cancers. I truly believe you work for something vitally important, not only for others, but possibly even for yourselves. **All of us can get cancer!**

OUR FORGOTTEN MILITARY PERSONNEL AND FAMILIES:

American men and women who serve our great country are looked upon by many who believe them to be lovers of war. Remember those wonderful people who marched in the '60s with that great peace symbol? During their march, they found it necessary to deface private and public property, destroying cars, setting fires, breaking store windows, stealing. Yeah, just your average peace-loving group from the '60s movement. These groups were led by someone who yelled into a microphone, "Baby killers," then the group of marchers would yell back, "Yeah, man, yeah." Then the soft-spoken leader would yell again, "Women killers." "Yeah, man, yeah." This was done during the conflict of the Vietnam (and Korean?) war. What was said by these great people who were "anti-something" was the word, "War, Vietnam War." I am not sugar-coating these issues.

Those of you Americans out there who do not understand the use of the word "war," better look back into time and you will understand what is war. War, 1, 2, 3, 4, and 5 thousand years ago, meant–burn everything, kill everyone and march on to the next village. But let us only go back, say 75 years. This information can easily be found. The use of poisonous gas, the V2 rockets into Britain; the German bombers destroying most all of eastern Europe, western Europe, and the Slavic countries; General Patton setting out into Germany, his tank and artillery guns firing into towns; when General Dwight D. Eisenhower, who commanded all the armies of Europe, called upon the Army Air Corps to bomb Germany back into the stone age (with F.D.R.'s blessing); when President Truman released two B29s to drop the first atomic bombs against Japan ... the thousands of men, women and innocent children that were killed. NOW THAT IS THE DEFINITION OF WAR. Whether we like it or not, that is HISTORY.

Moving on a few years and the problem of Korea and North Vietnam arises. This time in our great history, our leaders decide that "war is very bad." So what we do is called, "measured response." What that meant was, "to use an equal force." The results, as you have seen ... in Korea, Vietnam, Iraq and Afghanistan, are better known as a "never ending war."

Now we return to the title: the Forgotten Military. Our military personnel of the Korean and Vietnam conflicts have been mistreated, abused and basically forgotten by our leadership that goes back 50 years. But most of all what, we the people (including myself), have done is not given them their military benefits due to the "definition of conflict," not a declared war. Many suffer damage from the use of Agent Orange. Many military survivors have other war-related symptoms. I can't tell you about these items because I don't know about them. I do know that after speaking to a Vietnam veteran who drove trucks with supplies to the front lines, that he had strange symptoms that no one could diagnose. What is it, how did he get it, where, and when did he get it? Who knows? I do not know, other than to say, we have too many war vets who seem to suffer from something (PTSD?).

O.K. so off I go to do some basic research. Agent Orange's primary duty was to destroy plant life (Agent Orange: nickname of the defoliant used in Vietnam). That's easy, I use something similar very sparingly to eliminate weeds, before planting. So I read the label that says, "How to Use," the precautionary statements: *"Apply by spraying. Hazardous to humans and animals, causes eye irritation, avoid contact with the eyes, skin and clothing. Wash (clothing/skin contaminated areas) thoroughly with soap and water after handling. People and animals may enter the area after the spraying has dried."*

First thing I see here is that a soldier, in many instances, crawls around and walks through plants and trees contaminated with the defoliant. He cannot wash his hands or clothes with soap and water. Even the water may be contaminated with the same chemical. So what happened?

We cannot change history, but we can find out and fast. Do we know their families? Can they be affected? What about their children? Will it affect the fetus? I'm being pulled back into the problem itself, I cannot solve anything in that place. What can I do? I have way too many questions.

So let's issue an executive order. Bring in the folks at Fort Detrick (Army Medical Research) or the Center for Disease Control, bring in chemists from manufacturing–someone who has worked with plant elimination products. Someone out there must have some information.

Our Military Veterans, past and present have not been given the respect they deserve for their service to our country. I would like to see us give a big party throughout the nation in our stadiums and coliseums–a "Welcome Home Party." It should be a private party for Veterans and their families only. Politicians will not be welcome unless they too served. Senators McCain and Kerry and others within our government are included. (I will not attend. I was drafted, but failed the physical due to back problems.) Funds for this honorable event will come from donations and from Foreign Base closures. This event is 50 years overdue! The Military personnel and their families have been thrown away and forgotten.

Yes, we place memorials for those that died. They died without knowing the purpose of their deaths–because it was a conflict of politics and our leaders playing chess with the lives of our wonderful American soldiers. The dead, we place their names on our memorials, but the living received no "welcome home" or "thank you" for their duty and devotion honoring our country.

We, the people have forgotten what they gave up to preserve and protect us. We spend those commemorative holidays: Memorial Day, Veteran's Day, Independence Day, taking care of our own lives and families. Those holidays, plus Flag Day, Armed Forces Day, and Pearl Harbor Day were placed on our calendars to remind us who we are and to remember our Armed Forces–both past and present. When you go off on that vacation or three day holiday, stop a moment and give thanks for their sacrifice. Get an American Flag and fly it.

WHY ARE WE SELLING OUR CHILDREN?

The more I hear about how our adoption system works, the more I begin to wonder, where are the absolute locks to prevent the horror of the adoptive parents being caught in their worst nightmare?

I worked with a man who was married. He and his wife were childless and after many years decided to adopt a newborn child. They went to a highly accredited adoption center. It included a large law firm who mainly worked for the adoption center; a doctor on staff, etc. The papers were signed and the requirements were stated. For four months before the birth, the birth mother would live with the adoptive parents and also receive a two-year scholarship to be placed in a trust. All expenses would be paid by the adoptive parents.

When it came time for the newborn to be welcomed into the world, my friend and his wife almost slept at the hospital. The little boy arrived. The birth mother stayed one day and left. The little guy spent two more days at the hospital to make sure he was A-OK. He was given to his new parents who took him to his own room decorated with all types of sports figures. Everyone was happy, or so it would seem.

Three months later, a policeman and social worker show up at my friend's door and they remove the baby! He will be returned to his birth mother. A judge ruled that the child belonged to his birth mother! My friend and his wife were going crazy over the loss. She had to visit a psychiatrist or she would lapse into a complete mental breakdown. My friend stayed at work not quite a year and then left. I asked him what and where are you going? He told me that they were going to go to another country to adopt a child. He also said he paid a private investigator to find out what happened to the child and his birth mother. He found out that she had three children and lived in a tent outside the city. All three children had been adopted out and then returned to her. The whole thing was a sham. The law firm also knew of her previous games.

It cost my friend over $45,000 plus the Private Investigator's fee. Where is the sense in laws that allow someone to go through this type of hell?

ON PUBLIC EDUCATION:

I'll start out and say, how sad it is to have our children's future under the control of a political system. Teachers, education and politics DO NOT mix. The teaching profession is one of our most honorable, whereas Politics has little honor or ethics. Hopefully your grand parents, your parents, and your teacher taught you ethics in your early life and in grammar school. You as parents trust your most valuable treasure, your children, to teachers. Why do you (teachers) belong to Teacher's Unions? Is it their purpose to protect you or give themselves a job? Are they teachers or business bosses?

Teachers, years ago, taught us the use of books and materials as guides to learning. In the past 50 years, the administrators chose to have the teachers as a class monitor, the books in the classroom became the teacher. Teachers now have a rule book to follow and must keep track of attendance or the school will not be paid (money from the state). The school gets paid by a head count. Why not by graduating students with a minimum standards (or better)? The the reason you have joined a Union is so that all teachers get paid the same. I'll tell you right now that all teachers are not the created equal. Why should they all get paid equally? Seems to me that those that can teach and graduate students with at least the minimum standards in a ghetto area ought to be paid at a higher level than standard rural or upper class suburbia. It takes much more effort to recruit good teachers and to teach children who are under privileged and from drug-laced families in gang-prone areas. They should be the highest paid IF they can accomplish the job! Bonuses should be given to teachers who can raise the standard and produce more students *above* the average minimum. Let's base each teacher's salaries on his/her student's performance and a school's government money on the number of students graduating.

My mother taught school and she said that some teachers just show up and then go home–the children in that class take the hit. Then the school graduates the student to the next teacher who really has trouble with students who did not learn. He or she has to overcome that lack of understanding before presenting new material. So the whole class will, more than likely, be behind. The current system does not make it. Only ACTION can fix it.

TENURE–An educational disaster

Individuals who receive pay by doing nothing or as little as possible! Some people within our country seem to have elevated their status in life above others by receiving pay sometimes for life. What I see is, this idea stems from our English History background. The importance of Kings and Queens–a lifetime job. The idea is NOT AMERICAN!

We have college professors who, in many instances, do not show up for their classes, they have students run their class, in some cases writing the exams and correcting the exams.

In some classes a recorded session is used in lieu of the teacher. We pay for these teachers and their lack of ethics and I believe we even pay them a lifetime salary. This must be stopped!

Tenure is defined as, "the act or right of holding one's position permanently, as in a "tenured professor," who cannot be removed from his or her post except in extreme circumstances." These professors who taught and probably did a good job at one time, but perhaps they have lost their interest in teaching. The pros on Tenure reads like this: "Tenure makes original ideas more likely to arise, by giving scholars the intellectual autonomy to investigate the problems and solutions about which they are most passionate, and to report their honest conclusions." OK does that mean these research intellectuals should be teaching our students? They undoubtedly need to be writing books and papers on these problems and solutions at least.

Perhaps, we should give teachers of our very young children Tenure also, because these are the MOST IMPORTANT GROUP OF TEACHERS. They set in motion each child's beginning of learning, understanding and reasoning. We carry as adults, those time we spent as young people learning, remembering what you learned and remembering teacher's names.

I love them for those memories and what they gave me. All young children must be equipped with our basic learning concepts: English, Math and History, including the ability to write. If they do not understand those basics in life, those college professors will never see them.

Children need a very wide, solid base in which to grow. We have living testimony of this in our country, but most of all, within third world countries. It is clear that if you do not learn at an early stage, your future is doomed!

MILITARY COLLEGES

(Mandatory Changes)

I believe that Non-Americans should not be allowed entrance to our Military Colleges:

* United States Military Academy—West Point (est. 1802)
* United States Naval Academy—(est. 1845)
* United States Coast Guard Academy—(est. 1876)
* United States Merchant Marine Academy—(est. 1938)
* United States Air University—(est. 1946)
* United States Air Force Academy—(est. 1954)

There may be other Military Academies and Colleges that I am not familiar with–those also should be included in the list above. These military educations facilities were set up many years ago. They are now institutions, like our national monuments a part of our history. They involve America's duty, honor, and service to our country.

> *"It is an unfortunate fact that we can secure peace only by preparing for war."*
> John F. Kennedy

Lincoln's Gettysburg Address says it best. A portion of the address reads:

> ... *"We have come to dedicate a portion of that field, as a final resting place for those who here gave their lives that that nation might live. It is altogether fitting and proper that we should do this.*
>
> *But, in a larger sense, we can not dedicate—we can not consecrate—we can not hallow—this ground. The brave men, living and dead, who struggled here, have consecrated it, far above our poor power to add or detract. The world will little note, nor long remember what we say here, but it can never forget what they did here."* ...
>
> –President Abraham Lincoln

"Home is where the heart is"

quote: Gaius Plinius Secundus (Pliny the Elder)r)

I grew up in "homes," not "houses." I'll explain what I see as the difference. For me, a "home" is a place you go to– to see your grandparents. Let me describe it. The home is small and the furnishings are plain and well-used. When you walk in, the first thing you notice is the smell of food, all kinds of wonderful scents – fresh bread just out of the oven, maybe a leg of lamb or roast beef. The kitchen, dining and living room are all together. My grandmother Mailho would always have three or four roast chickens. Inside the chickens, she would place small pieces of sourdough french bread. The outside was rubbed with garlic. One chicken would have fresh rosemary inside and another shallots. You walked in to the dining room to a very large dining table. The plates, sitting by the oven, would be warm and the flatware was a mix of many brands. Glasses were all mixed sizes and shapes and some even had chips. It made no difference. On the table was a very large salad bowl, almost 20" in diameter. Inside the bowl was butter lettuce, chicory, romaine lettuce, tomatoes of different types and lots of vegetables from my grandpa's garden. The smell of wine vinegar, my grandfather made his own vinegar and used olive oil from an Italian friend. Grandfather always said Grace. He always stated how grateful he was for all the farmers who brought food to all of us.

My mother followed that idea of people gathered around the table, family and friends. My wife Linda, follows that idea today. However, she does one thing differently, she even grinds the wheat berries to flour, such fresh flour. The pastas, breads and all the baked goods are outstanding. One day in August of this year (2007), I received a call from her, one of many calls. Since she is in Florida and I'm in California, she calls me about three times a day. She said, "I'm baking cookies today, would you like some?" I said, "yes, but I can't get there now." Two days later a FedX truck arrived at the door with package for me. I open the box and inside, in sealed bags, were different types of cookies. The box was named "Care Mail, a taste of home."

To many of you out there, you may have missed having my home life. If today, right now you live in a "house," you can easily change it into a "home." Step into your house with goodness and wonderful thoughts, spend time with those you love, place your heart within all things you do and your surroundings will be a "home."

FEEDING THE CHILDREN:

On the topic of feeding our children–or should it be feeding the world's children, who seem always to be at the brink of starvation? Humans love to always blame someone else for the problem, but never looking at one's self. I said earlier that Americans have given their time and money to support, HELP, whatever to foreign countries. We've given food, built schools, places of worship, medical teams, etc. Everything they've done is extremely honorable, I have no gripe with what they did. Except that these Americans, somehow, drove a car, or flew to these areas to help. In doing so they flew over, walked by and drove through areas within our country with the same problems. The people within our country, you know, the unmentionables that we do not want to admit to. We have some serious problems within our country and do not address, know or care about them.

I turned on my C Band satellite TV and picked up a Chicago Station on Saturday. A program was on called "Feed the Children." On the screen showed children. Their faces were like the faces I see at our school yard in Sonora (California). My God, these were American children. The man was speaking about the forgotten children in America. Thousands? Who actually knows? The first thing that came to my mind was, "Oh, boy, another sham (scam) group." You know what I'm saying. Slow down, Bob, and hear the man out. On and on he spoke and then he said the magic words, "If we do not feed them, who will?" That's it! That sentence indicates a problem and ends with a challenging question ... "Who will?" I could tell you who won't and I will not tell you the answer because it is so plain to see. The program on TV was from some group in the US, and I believe they have good intentions. However, I would prefer to go and speak with them in person. The organization is from the great "sooner" state of Oklahoma.

On T.V. and in my mailbox I get "junk mail" from organizations asking for money to feed children. On T.V. you see Christian foundations showing children from foreign nations mainly from south of our borders or Africa–on and on it goes. This topic really pisses me off "big time." The United States has given millions of dollars in aid for such problems. This issue is perhaps the greatest sham ever (However, I know these children are truly in need). Why is it that these nations that we continue to give aid to have made no progress in their nation? Well, it's quite simple, you see. Perhaps 10% or less of the food is given to the needy, the rest is sold by that nation to other nations! You must understand that these countries know we will continue to give them more and more, more–the never-ending game.

We, as Americans have a foolish notion of going out of our way to help everyone in the world, except here at home. Do you really believe you will make a tremendous difference? Unfortunately not. You do not have the power to change that government, because it is not *your* government! You can come back home and say and feel very good about yourself, you definitely deserve that. But the feelings (and effects) are short-lived. Unless you live next door to them in that country and continue giving for the rest of your life, which you probably won't. So when you leave them it goes back to the way it was. Someone tells me, "I believe in the United Nations, they will pick up the gauntlet and carry on your crusade." Good luck people.

If you truly believe that the "all saving" United Nations, which I believe to be the largest group of despots will help the general poor and starving, you are a delusional individual. If you were born when the UN was formed, you would now be able to collect your Social Security. Can you tell me what the United Nations has truly done, I'm saying all the members participating as a United Nations group? From my limited knowledge, you will not find a UN group participating in anything. What you will find is the good ole U.S.A. putting its finger into the fire again and again. Plus there are a handful of other nations also. The only agreement that is unanimous is the lunch bell or dinner, that's my take on it.

As you have noticed, I do not like the atmosphere of the United Nations. In fact, I would like them to move their headquarters operation building to another nation. My grandfather would love me for suggesting the country of choice–France. "The city of lights, all roads lead to Paris," etc. Besides since we no longer have the World Trade Center, why not move the U.N. headquarters elsewhere? Just think, you New Yorkers, the relief of less traffic and less smog. Have the WTC rebuilt in Japan. It will give the main architects a chance to build it the way they wanted. The architects that designed the WTC did a great job. However, the ever-present politicians wanted more from the building and so we see what happened. Remember politicians know all and see all. But in reality they know nothing and do nothing. I would say this, if we were to be part of the UN, we should do so by being more passive, meaning we do not jump each time a problem around the world comes up. We must allow the other *esteemed* assembly participants to really step up to the plate and play.

This is the 21st century. For the past 90 years, the United States of America has held up to the world. Remember, Atlas, the world on his shoulders? That's us. Here we are, the youngest *major* nation on earth (third largest in number of people), about 230 years old. Whereas many other nations (other than a name change) may go back into time as far as 5,000 years ago or more! People of America it's time to allow someone else to carry the weight of the world. The world's problems, to suffer the blood loss, the criticism of whatever we do, good, bad or otherwise, it will always be wrong.

AMERICANS TAKING CARE OF AMERICANS:

Not long ago, a family and members of its church went on a crusade to Mexico. This was not the first time. That family has been going every year for 3 generations of their family. They travel south and build homes, school buildings, etc. A truly noble deed–and I respect them very much. However, I understand we Americans are perhaps the only culture who is always helping others in many ways. Somehow it must be in our bones, because we continue to support others less fortunate. My wife, Linda, and I have given a great deal of food to Food Banks in our area. One year my wife donated over 2000 pounds of food during the holidays. We believe it did get to the people in need in our county. Our home in Copperopolis, California has a school of the old fashioned style. Different grades all in one classroom. The teachers are very good. Can you imagine teaching different grades in one room? Most all of the students are from very poor families, so Christmas is going to be slim. Linda, my treasure, went to the school and told the Principal her plan. He could not help her with information because of some confidentiality law. He suggested that she talk to the local Reverend of the church. She did and he gave her the students first name and a last letter initial, age, sex, what they like, etc. Now she had what she needed. She asked me if it would be O.K. if I did not buy her a Christmas present that year. "If that's what you want," I said. Then she told me what she wanted to do. I asked her, "What about the (childrens') parents?" She went back to the Reverend and asked if it would be O.K. to give him envelopes with vouchers from local stores, clothing, pharmacys. He could then distribute them to the parents in need and not give her name. The Reverend agreed. She asked the teacher for the names of the rest of the students in the class so everyone would receive a gift.

The day before Christmas vacation, I helped her load our truck with this huge sack of presents. The sack was as large as a king-size bed. She put on her Santa outfit and off she went. She arrived at recess time. The Reverend was there and had Linda drive right up to the school door. It was her day. Boy, was it a day–one she'll never forget. The bag was so big it was difficult to get through the door. The children really wanted that bag inside the class room, so they formed a human wall. The teacher told the children to take their seats. She also had a seating chart. Linda would pull out a present, walk to the teacher's desk, glance down at the chart to find the child's name. Then she then could go to each child and say, "this one belongs to you" and say their name. She had different stickers on the packages which indicated which class and the names on the packages. Many of the students received more than one gift.

What Linda and I do is like many other Americans. However, there are very few who give more than gifts and time. Each day these group of Americans put their lives on the line–their devotion to duty first. They protect the lives of children always first. The Fire personnel and their comrades, the Paramedics, who rush to administer to those in need. Cars or buildings on fire–they rush to save children and adults they have never met. People who save people. What an incredible spirit! The fireman rushes into buildings on fire—tall buildings ablaze. Police are always ready to respond. However, they have a terrible set of rules to play the game by. Those rules allow too many police personnel to be killed each year–and for what? On 9/11/01, I saw on television people running for their lives. Everyone was the color of gray. Then the camera picked up the fireman and police running toward the buildings on fire, running to save people they didn't know. Many of them died too.

Some years back there was a barracks with soldiers in their bunks. Someone outside the entrance to the barracks pulled the pin on a grenade and threw it inside. Many of the men were asleep, some were reading, one soldier saw the grenade roll past him. At that moment, he decided that the grenade was not going to kill his comrades in arms. He ran and jumped onto the grenade so that his body protected his fellow soldiers. Some would say that he was "Horatius at the Bridge (an English poem of valor)." No, I don't believe so. For years I have studied many instances of men and women sacrificing themselves to protect others. I believe it has nothing to do with sacrifice. No, it's something else. One of our built-in protection devices–very strong is self-preservation. No, most of us would not knowingly kill ourselves to save anyone else. It goes beyond that. I believe they instantly set in their minds to protect someone from death and by doing so defeat death–and we all will live. If you know you will live, it cancels the self-preservation instinct.

Perhaps, probably not, this breed of protectors of people, are mostly descended from a culture that stems back to the great Celtic peoples–the same family who gave us bronze. The Irish, Scottish and Welsh today are from this family culture. If you ever see a funeral procession you will notice a pipe player–a bag pipe with a kilt worn from time's past. The Scottish and Irish today have found a home within our American culture.

There are no words that can ever describe such instances of heroism. WWII had hundreds of these instances. Our present Secret Service is such a group who live with this all the time. We have Greatness here, people.

For those of you who think you are so important–and those who do not ...

WHO WE ARE AND THE IMPORTANCE WE ALL HAVE

I was walking by WalMart the other day. A man about my age was cleaning the garbage off the sidewalk where it met the building wall. I watched him for a moment. Then smiled to myself and walked over to him and said, "Do you know that if it was necessary to perform a major operation at this point in time, I would say, the way you cleaned that sidewalk would pass inspection as an auxiliary operating table." He smiled and said, "No one has ever told me I did a good job." I know, it seems that very few people give anyone a compliment on a job well done. "What did you do before this job?" I asked. "I installed diffusion furnaces back east." "Oh, OK, I said, "I know about diffusion furnaces. If you were asked, What job was more important, what would you say?" He said, "Both jobs are the same, they are equally important." Surprised, I stood there for a moment and then told him, "that's the first time I have ever heard anyone say, 'all jobs are equally important.'"

OK, I hear some doubt out there. Let's take a surgeon, now that's a very important job. I believe we will agree about that. Now, we are going to wheel you into the operating room. I'm assuming you are still awake. Take a look around the room and see all that equipment. Lots of it. Take a quick glance at the women in green bringing over a tiny tray made of stainless steel.

There is a white cloth, looks like a dish towel, but it isn't. The nurse folds back the "dish towel" and before your eyes are the most beautiful tools. You'll never see those in your auto store. If you are truly lucky, you may see an obsidian scalpel (volcanic glass).

The surgical nurse is extremely important. Doctors rely on them because the nurse is the tool master. She knows how the operation is progressing, gives the doctor, on key, the instrument required before he asks. Most doctors will not work unless he has with him his surgical nurse. And, the team members, you see everyone in that room is important–very important. At one time I wanted to be a surgeon. However, I felt it was too repetitious. So, I went back to engineering and developing all kinds of things. That's what I feel, I was born to do.

I've only spoken to you about the people in an operating room and their importance to the doctors. Now the success of the operation is in all the members of that team. What I'm trying to project, is the *importance* of each and every person. Remember when you entered the O.R. and saw the equipment? Consider all the tens of thousand of people who made that equipment! The tools ... Let's go way back to the men who mined the minerals for the equipment, the equipment the miners used, the ore transportation. Jumping ahead to the smelting of the ore–men standing by the furnaces at temperatures above 2,500o degrees and the man's clothing or protection suit. The protective clothing, now we're talking a whole new industry that includes thousands of more people and on it goes. I could write ten or more pages about just how one tool was made–that tool so very important to the doctor. But you will never hear about all those people who made that operation a reality.

After your operation, orderlies come into the room and a team leader. In some cases, a highly trained nurse whose job it is to insure the the cleanliness of the operating room you just left. The orderlies do the grunt work, they know the importance of what they are doing. An orderly is not paid much for the his or her job. However, what they do is extremely important to the doctor and staff. You see, if they do not do a superior job you, the patient, may be subjected to extreme levels of viruses and bacteria. The doctor's worst nightmare is infection.

If you go to any hospital to visit a patient or groups of patients, always enter their room and put a small amount of anti-bacterial solution on your hands before you enjoy your stay. If you have a cold or are getting over one, go to the front desk and tell them you are just getting over a cold and ask for a mask. The hospital will appreciate you for protecting their patients. All of this information comes under the heading of Humanitarianism and Common Sense. Next time you visit your friend at the hospital, if you see an orderly mopping the floors, go to the them and thank them. You just might make their day. No, I'm *sure* you will!

HISTORY PAST AND PRESENT:

I read a magazine that spoke of our history of the Civil War between the Yankees and the Rebels. What this article was about is how each year actors, players (soldiers) of that time frame, act out the different battles of our Civil War. Many of these players are ancestors of the soldier they play and are celebrating their heritage. Many teachers of history join in to better understand what it may have been like to fight in those battles. A very difficult task indeed. Most of the players attempt to place themselves inside the body and mind of the person whom they are recreating. Why did they do this? Who were the Blue or Grey Coats (Americans all) who died on these battlefields? If you ever get the opportunity to visit a battlefield sit down on the grass, look around then close your eyes and try to picture yourself and place yourself back in time (one day I will do this). President Lincoln's immortal words describe it best (The Gettysburg Address). Those men of honor and greatness who died because of an idea fought here. The idea is within our Constitution: Life, Liberty and Freedom for all. We are all equal–so brothers killed brothers. So once again the idea of liberty must be renewed with blood.

Our country has always been strong. Now and then, we slip up slightly, but we always come back far more powerful. At this point in time, I would say we have slipped. Our schools have forgotten how to teach. The profession of teaching, which is ruled by administrators, shows a total lack of political responsibility in many areas of our great land. Why is education a political thing? It is our most important task! More important that just a strong military. We seem to live in a throw-away society. We throw away generation after generation of the young. We throw away our citizens by our in-action to protect them. We destroy families, towns, and jobs, and import goods and export manufacturing to the point that other countries will catch up with us.

OUR TRADE DEFICIT AND TRADING ALLOWANCES:

Our country imposes many regulations and controls over our food producers, which may make our food safer, but makes operating a small business almost impossible. Government personnel who know nothing about the business of ranching and farming, have now become the *experts*. The experts in somebody's life which they now control. "Life, liberty and the pursuit of happiness ..." now do not apply.

(www.ers.usda.gov/publications/err30/).

We have large quantities of agricultural products stored–going nowhere. At the same time, people in foreign nations around the world are starving. I read that there are over 70 countries with whom we have trade embargoes. (See the Selective Embargoes Act of 1998). I do not know who these countries are, but I'll put that aside for now. However, what better way to reach out and set up some form of trade, even with those countries with which we have some form of disagreement? Each of those countries must have something to trade with us.

Thinking back as a little boy, I remember the Christian faith doctrine of sharing bread with anyone. In the Muslim world these are the ideas of the *Pillars of Hospitality*. This type of policy (of food restrictions) does our country absolutely no good. In distributing food goods, we give up nothing, not our sovereignty nor our security, nor does it instill a weakness in the culture of the United States. People, we are not trading guns here!

Some of our trading partners are playing a game of "I win, you America lose." Japan, as an example: we supply beef to them. Japan is not a heavy producer of cattle on their crowded home islands. Japan places a tariff of 40% on us for beef imports. I know for a fact that a steak in Japan can cost you up to $200 a la carte (American dollars). So for the average citizen to order beef in Japan is non existent. So we are not going up against their own producers, as in Canada.

Canada imposes a tariff of 35% on poultry and dairy products from us. I thought we formed NAFTA (North American Free Trade Agreement) to eliminate tariffs between our country and Canada and Mexico. A law suit was filed by the U.S.A. The WTO (World Trade Organization) ruled that countries may impose tariffs to protect their domestic producers. Now we understand why NAFTA has been a great blessing. We, as Americans, cannot and will not be pulled into this imbalance of trade due to foreign nations self-preservation of its own people–to hell with us. No way.

We need to redo all of the US trade agreements with all nations. The playing field needs to be level. One way to do this is what I call, "mirror image." As an example, if Japan, per say, was trading products they produce we would add a 40% tariff to products from Japan. The tariff of 40% against us for beef does not injure its home product, but should be considered a blessing to their country because it would reduce the over-fishing of all our oceans.

The same applies to China. Now I cannot blame foreign nations for this problem. I put the blame right on our lobbyists in the State Department. People who draw up these agreements, there is the true enemy.

WARS:

Our Civil War was a terrible waste of American lives on both sides. I have a hard time seeing a winner or loser in this conflict because it was a war against one's brothers. We retained one nation under one rule and a beginning to end slavery, but there is no North or South to me. The incredible sadness President Lincoln must have felt, shows in the words so beautifully spoken in his Gettysburg address. That is, in my opinion, the second greatest speech ever spoken by anyone.

President Wilson did not want to enter World War I. "That's for the Europeans to settle." However, the American people wanted to help and he was asked to support Europe against the Germans. What I don't know is who put the actual pressure on the President. Did we have those wonderful lobbyists then? Perhaps this was their beginning. The blood of Americans was spilt all over the continent. Many died not knowing the real reason they were fighting. At that period in time we somehow became the force of liberty and freedom for all–the police force of the world. At the end of the war President Wilson his war aims in his famous Fourteen Points speech, with the last point calling for the creation of a League of Nations. The war itself was labeled, "the war to end all wars." What a stupid statement!

World War II–here we go again! Germany did not like the treaty they signed after WWI, so came back with a war machine that the world had never seen. During that time, the countries of Europe were asleep. Franklin Delano Roosevelt did not wish to enter that war either. Someone convinced Franklin Delano Roosevelt to supply war goods to our wonderful allies in Europe. However, there was a catch. The U.S.A. was to "lend lease" the war materials and the receivers must pay us back. Did we ever get any payments for these war goods? I have not seen any information on the answer to this question.

Germany did not invade our country, but Japan did. We sent our "police force" into the war on the European continent once again. We could have shortened the war on the Eastern front and saved thousands of soldiers lives, but politics said, "Oh no, we can't do that." That's when politics began to determine the outcome and the course of military conflicts. As a result, F.D.R., Stalin, and Churchhill made some type of pact and the US troops were held back to allow Stalin to enter Germany. Bad precedent. So as we march ahead a new conflict emerges. The "Cold War" begins. General Patton was right in his assessments and the politicians were wrong again.

Japan was way ahead in the war when they invaded our islands. I remember in 1970, when I returned from my yacht trip that some of the members were talking about someone writing a letter to the editor of the the newspaper in San Diego. It was in reference to a letter F.D.R. wrote that was to be opened 25 years after his death. These rumors were from WWII vets and they stated that F.D.R. knew about the coming invasion before it happened. I have not seen any such letter. It smells of politics again.

Remember:

If you want peace, prepare for war.
Victory belongs to those who believe the most.
We will not give in.

TRIBES AND SLAVES:

For the last three years I have gone back 600 years into our history. The purpose was to find out why the world and our country is still in turmoil. What I found out was, the world, including us, is run by tribes. Tribes can be described by their: language and/or dialect, race, culture, facial appearance (tribal markings), religion, status in life, and beliefs and political ideas. Each day on T.V. you will witness many of these tribal antics that separate us as a country and prevent *E Pluribus Unum*, as it were.

During WWII we, as a country, were separated by race and facial appearance from each other on our own front. During the Vietnam "Conflict," our soldiers were truly the "Band of Brothers" and tribal differences were buried for the most part. Today we are brnging back our old tribal conflicts once again. Why?

If you see any nation today and trace the history of their tribe, you can see just what country they originated from. I used 600 years ago because that was one of the greatest periods of migration of people throughout the world that the human race has seen. The question is, what was the mission these men were given when they found land fall? The answer is quite clear in history, to raid, plunder, loot and assume power, or at least a presence, if possible in the name of their country.

Send back treasure to the parent country and set up and establish a colony. In many cases, to use the people of the country invaded as slaves to their own needs. Lands of conquest were Central and South America, Africa, Mexico, the islands of the Caribbean and other islands of the Pacific. The Inca and Mayan cultures were decimated by disease and death.

Recorded history dates slave markets 5,000 years ago in Egypt and China, followed by the Romans, Turks, Syrians and the list goes on. Japan used slave labor in building fortresses and Chinese and American prisoners from the Philippines were used all during WWII. Germany used nations conquered for building fortresses throughout Europe until 1944. So slavery is not a new thing, nor ending with us, as it continues today. Slavery, as we knew it in America, has been abolished. In essence it continues in our inner cities with American citizens being controlled by drug lords, pimps and gang leaders.

Africa is the only country we hear of today in a tribal sense. A day does not go by in which someone blames all their troubles on America. Africa was a land of tribes and tribal wars long before we began to take their peoples as slaves. In Africa, one tribe still captures and kills another and uses them even now as they did back in the 1400s. During that time, slavers sold the native peoples of that land for all kinds of items, and to locations all over Europe. In the 1700s, slaves were brought to America in slaving ships from Africa, Spain, Portugal and France. They unloaded their "cargo" (what a horrible word for the life of a human being) in our southern states.

I'm going to tell you of a man I worked with who was born and raised in Mississippi. His parents, were farmers who lived along the banks of that great river. A small group of us were having lunch and this co-worker was talking about how his great, great, grandparents were slaves and how bad it was for them. My partner pounded his fist upon the table and said, "You do not know what you're talking about. Yes, our forefathers were slaves. However, that was a very long time ago. I'm so happy that my ancestors were sold into slavery in this country, in the United States of America. I'll tell you why: because if they were not, I would not be here today. Africa still seems to be a slave country and if you do not believe that, the Africans you call your brothers and sisters are killing each other at an unbelievable rate today. During our lunch time, 5,000 or more will be killed outright or starve to death, while you sit there and eat your lunch. America has sent to Africa 100s of tons of food and most of that does not reach the people. Your black brothers take it and sell it on the Black Market instead. America is not the problem, the Africans are the problem! And I want you to stop calling yourself an African American, because that word means "racism." It indicates a person's race. I am an American and always will be." At that moment, I remembered my grandfather's statement, "I was born in France, but I am an American." I stood up, reached across the table and shook his hand. I said, "How great it is for me to shake the hand of a real American."

HAS THE MIDDLE EAST EVER BEEN STABLE?

We talk about "de-stabilization" quite a bit. In the last few years it seems that it is always pointed at the U.S. During the beginning of the first Gulf War, the U.N. Security Council drug its feet for days placing all those ultimatums in place to convince Sadam to stop the invasion of Kuwait and return to his own lands. Days and days went by while Sadam continued to march south. Finally the Council's last ultimatum was delivered and still the idea of stopping Sadam was held off because someone said Israel may be a *de-stabilizing* force in the region. The U.S.A.

told Israel to back off. We placed Patriot Missile batteries in place to shoot down SCUD missiles. Sadam's "immortals tanks" drove into Kuwait and killed everyone in sight. Finally the O.K. was given to push Sadam back across the Kuwait border only. The U.S. was not the only nation to fight this battle. Sadam must have missed getting birthday candles on his cake as a boy, because he instructed that all the oil fields in Kuwait be torched and blown apart at the well heads. Good one, Sadam. It was estimated that it would take five to seven years to put out those fires that he caused. In fact, a couple of months later, I heard on the news that some company had managed to put out the fires on these wells in Kuwait. That was the best news. The fires burning were really causing havoc in the atmosphere and all that oil floating in the air soon had to settle back down to earth ...

Back to my point. People of the United States should realize that the Middle East, as we call it, has been at war forever. There hasn't been any kind of peace there through most of history, back as far as Biblical times. That area has no living people who know what peace means.

Wars and Battles of the Middle East*	
War Name	**Date(s)**
Egyptian Invasion of Asia	1479 bc
Persia Empire Wars	546 - 539 bc
Persian-Greek Wars	499 - 401 bc
Alexander & Macedonian Conquests	338 - 322 bc
Hellenistic Monarchies, Wars of the	318 - 170 bc
Third Macedonian War	168 bc
First Triumvirate, Wars of the	53 - 45 bc
Second Triumvirate, Wars of the	43 - 31 bc
Byzantine Empire Wars	395 - 1453
Muslim Conquests	624 - 982
The Crusades	1096 - 1254
Arab-Israeli War	1948 - 1949
Suez War	1956
Wars in Lebanon	1958 - 1983
Six-Day War	1967
October War	1973
Iran-Iraq War	1980 - 1988
Persian Gulf War	1991
War on Terror	2001-?

*Web reference: ehistory.osu.edu/middleeast/battles

They have never experienced it, except perhaps in remote and isolated areas. Granted we got involved in the last two wars. But even the most recent, the Iran-Iraq War went on for eight continuous years. How many people were killed? For what? The leaders of these nations could care less, it is their way of life! What makes us think we could go in and come even close to stabilizing the area? It's absurd!

The word *de-stabilization* is always used to indicate what we in America might or might not do during the "police Action" in Iraq now occurring. De-stabilize the Middle East? Has there ever been a stable time in history when these countries were friends? Good neighbors do not fight religious wars. Their Koran speaks of Holy Wars, but it refers to the attack on their religion. Now if I understand that sentence, they, the very few terrorists, are fighting a war that goes against their "so called" Muslim beliefs. They are killing vast amounts of good Islamic people. Why? Well, someone, somewhere over there in the Middle East is financing a Holy War against their own people. Just like it did 5,000 years ago. Someone has deemed that the wars, long past, are not finished!

If I was concerned about Middle East problems, I would look VERY carefully into the repeated problems of war in Gaza. As an example, do you remember a woman, I believe a Palestinian, (also part of the U.N.) repeating the phrase over and over again–"occupation, occupation?" She was referring to Israel holding ground taken during the Six-Day War in 1967. Almost the entire Middle Eastern Islamic people attacked Israel with no warning. Sounds familiar, i.e. 1941. Israel fought back and took land from Lebanon and other areas. The armies of the Islamic countries were defeated. Now, the word "defeated" means something different to all peoples. To the Islamic rulers and armies, this word means, "will rise again–to be continued, etc." This was quite evident in the Iran-Iraq War and in the Gulf War. When the armies of the "immortals" were overtaken, the first thing they do is shoot their weapon once and put it over their heads. If the army was American, who defeated you, we would not shoot anyone who surrenders. Now if these were two Islamic nations, the soldier who raised his weapon over his head, would give a quick prayer to Allah and would then be shot. The code of engagement and ethics in the Middle East are very different than ours (why we can't understand that is truly baffling!). We come under, by mutual agreement, the Geneva Convention code of war–a different culture than theirs. What I'm trying to portray is that those soldiers who gave up after the first and second wars in Iraq are back at it inside Iraq today. They live to fight!

In regard to that Palestinian woman speaker whose words were, "occupation, occupation," the point is, that Israel has been out of those territories that she was screaming about for at least one to two years. The Palestinians are free to build their independent state. But they have not and the war continues on and on with Arabs killing Arabs, Hamas and Fatah killing one another. Hamas loyal to Ismael Haniyeh continue to keep up the bloodletting for generation after generation by teaching very young children to hate and commit murders. The Hamas educational system, their television and every means possible, teaches them that suicide is a way of life. Parents are pictured crying with happiness after their children have committed suicide as a human bomb. To them those children are now sitting by Allah's hand. Why is it that this Palestinian woman speaker is no longer on TV? What is she going to say now? Israel is the problem!

The one issue in America that frequently comes up is that question, "Did Sadam Hussein actually have weapons of mass destruction?" This issue will continue to make news due to one's political ideals–for or against W.M.D.s. We do know that, by news reports, that W.M.D.s were used in northern Iraq principally in the Kurdish-held territories. If we can agree that the news media did not manufacture this story, and if it's true, my question is, from where, and how did the chemicals, equipment and technology get to Sadam's chemists? The news report found the equipment in bunkers. I believe that the bunkers were built by German engineering. The equipment came from Germany and France. Did those two countries put boots on the ground during the Gulf War? The U.N. Security Council certainly took a great deal of time before the switch was thrown to actually attack

Sadam. Is it possible that during those delays, Sadam may have moved his arsenal of W.M.D.s to, say Syria or Iran? We know Sadam's family moved to Syria. Within the U.N. Security Council, Sadam had alliances with most all members of the Middle East, including many members of Europe. The Europeans could easily be greased for information and thus allowed Sadam to move his W.M.D.s. Just because we did not find them does not mean that they do not exist!

You remember Eric Rudolf, the American terrorist? (Olympic Park Bomber) It took the U.S. from 1996 to 2003 to finally capture him. He was placed on America's Most Wanted list from 1998 to 2003 before his arrest. With all the resources available to the FBI in our own country, we spent years in his manhunt. It certainly seems possible to me that Sadam could have disposed of (moved?) his W.M.D.s *before* we ever started our "War on Terror" in Iraq.

THE PROBLEM OF OIL:

Our dependence upon oil is both good and bad. For many years oil has changed our economy to become one of the greatest influences in all fields. However, its downside is pollution, contribution to global warming, and dependence upon foreign countries.

But oil is not the only "bad guy" in global ozone depletion. Also contributing is the double effect of forest fires of huge magnitude. Besides the loss of valuable timber (slowing the creation of natural oxygen), natural resources and wildlife, fire creates a massive amount of pollution and dumps it directly into our atmosphere.

But we are stuck with oil and oil products for a while. Our government has placed benchmarks for auto manufacturing to comply with standards that reduces our fuel usage per vehicle. This is OK, a start, but with a rise in the number of vehicles on the roads that savings is totally pushed aside. Not only will manufacturers of vehicles eventually hit a wall in efficiency, the

American people may need to sacrifice horse power for fuel economy.

So what do we do? Electric cars may not be the answer as they must be charged up and plugged into a power grid somewhere. Remember charging batteries? Hybrid cars, blending the gasoline and electric (battery) power is a good combination, but a very complex piece of machinery. From my viewpoint, as taught by my mentors–design with simplicity. My dinosaur thinking is to always do things simply.

General Motors has what they call a "fuel flex" design. I believe from what I've been told, that this design is capable of using different types of fuel. So I called our local G.M. dealer in Jamestown, California and asked to speak to the person who knows about the fuel flex application. I asked him, "How much pure ethanol can your cars burn?" He replied, "Up to 85% without changing anything." A computer senses the fuel type and amount and adjusts the engine to run on that type of fuel. Using ethanol we may burn more fuel. The more ethanol we burn (replacing gasoline), the less polution we create, the less oil we require and thus reduce our dependence foreign oil supplies. Yes, we will use more fuel, but it is renewable and we control it. THIS IS A KEY ELEMENT TO AMERICA'S PROGRESS. We must do this for America!

One important note: what I am suggesting is not the end game?–the Utopian fix. This is only an intermediate step to the future. The future fuel is out there to be discovered and utilized. I'm sure there are chemists and scientists working, searching for it now. You see, gasoline is to be the fuel of our past. I know our current fuel producers, refineries etc. will not like us to increase the use of ethanol. But those same industries need to be at the forefront of the search for an alternative that is universally acceptable, both environmentally and economically. These companies have made huge profits, "killings on the market." When prices of crude oil barrels are up, as announced by the media, so prices at the pumps go up. The tankers with the higher pricer oil have not left the dock yet! They are probably still using supplies from our current stores purchased at the lower levels. Now that's what I call a "real" ripoff!

AUTOS FROM THE '50s TO 2007 and OUR EVER-DWINDLING ENERGY FUEL SUPPLY

Since 1950 to mid 1960s fuel was in abundance. We built cars of that time to show the world what America was all about. The engines were monsters and I loved them!

Chrysler with their Hemi 300 series, Ford with their Mustangs with 427 engines, Chevys with their 265 cu-in V8s. They ran their engines short stroke, big bore allowed them to run at higher engine speeds–up to 5,500 RPMs. I ran my Chevy engine in 1956 with a modified engine that I built–at up to 8,000 RPM. Ohhh the sound of that engine …

When the '70s began, a hard lesson hit us all, reality. In 1973 we had to wait in line to buy gas and only to buy it on certain days. Some stations were allowed only so many gallons to be sold. The reason was that we were low on crude oil supplies. I do not know just how true this explanation was. Governments and major corporations have been known to distort the truth to do whatever it is they have in mind–whatever direction they wish to move you. Our history has shown that members of our Senate have created these distortions to promote their own agendas.

According to the history of Howard Hughes, in the late '40s, the senate committees tried to destroy Howard Hughes. For what? Politics? Preston Tucker built a very good automobile with safety features not found on any auto at that time. A senator destroyed him also. Tucker and Hughes were abstract thinkers, inventors always are. The senator did not want progress.

During the '50s, Germany introduced the economy VW or "Volkswagen" to the US. The car was "not worth a damn," the Ford representatives criticized. But it became so popular do to the ease of operation and low cost to operate (30 MPG) that during the 1960s and early 1970s, although the car was becoming outdated, its growing reputation for reliability helped production figures to surpass the levels of the previous record holder, the Ford Model T. By 1973, total production was over 16 million.

During the 1970s, Japan introduced their very small economy cars into the US market. The Datsun 1600. Compared to the 2000 versions, these cars were very fast, steering was hard and the rear suspension very hard. Most people did not go for this style as they were not what we could call "a family car." The Japanese went to a design firm to design them a car that Americans would like. I believe, in this case, it was the Art Center School of Design in Los Angeles, California. With this design the Japanese hit the target for a great car—the 240 Z. Fuel use was OK and the design was beautiful.

Other small cars from European and Japanese manufacturers made their debut on the American market. What is the biggest problem is that we, in America, did not really see the hand writing on the wall, so to speak. Back in the 60s and 70s we seemed to be in control of our destiny. We produced most of the fuel that we used. But our love of the large auto with the oversized engine that guzzles gasoline, and multiple autos per family, has caused a shortage in fuel production that makes us dependent upon foreign countries for oil. So today we are at the mercy of our "allies" so to speak. American manufacturers are finally coming to realize that fuel economy and mainly reliability are the most important factors in auto purchases. These realizations have come too late and have allowed the Japanese vehicles to become more popular in the US than the American autos. Our future is not good, as I see it. So we have to do something today and not wait like we have since the late '70s. The hand writing was on the wall then and we, all of us, stood around and did nothing. Like we did in the past–we will return to the past 1973 all over again.

So are we going to put more pressure on our auto makers to save us from this shortage of fuel? They don't control fuel production, but they cause the gasoline supply and demand to be excessive by making autos that get poor fuel milage. Does

America have the guts to change our ways again? So who are you goint to speak to about the lack of fuel? Our auto leaders? They have had over 30 years to figure out that we can burn different types of fuel. How will we survive our loss of fuel? For me, I'm going to buy for my next car, a hybrid that can burn different types of fuel, mainly ethanol. I would like to speak to our farmers–our fuel farmers. They will save us like they have been for all of our lives producing our crops.

I see different types of fuels: fossil fuels, propane, natural gas, kerosene, diesel, coal, vegetable oil, steam, solar panels, wind, and hydrogen. All can work, although some will not work in some locations (latitudes).

Solar power will work best at the equator, not as well at more northern latitudes. Perhaps wind? The diagram below illustrates a better way to allocate fuel ...

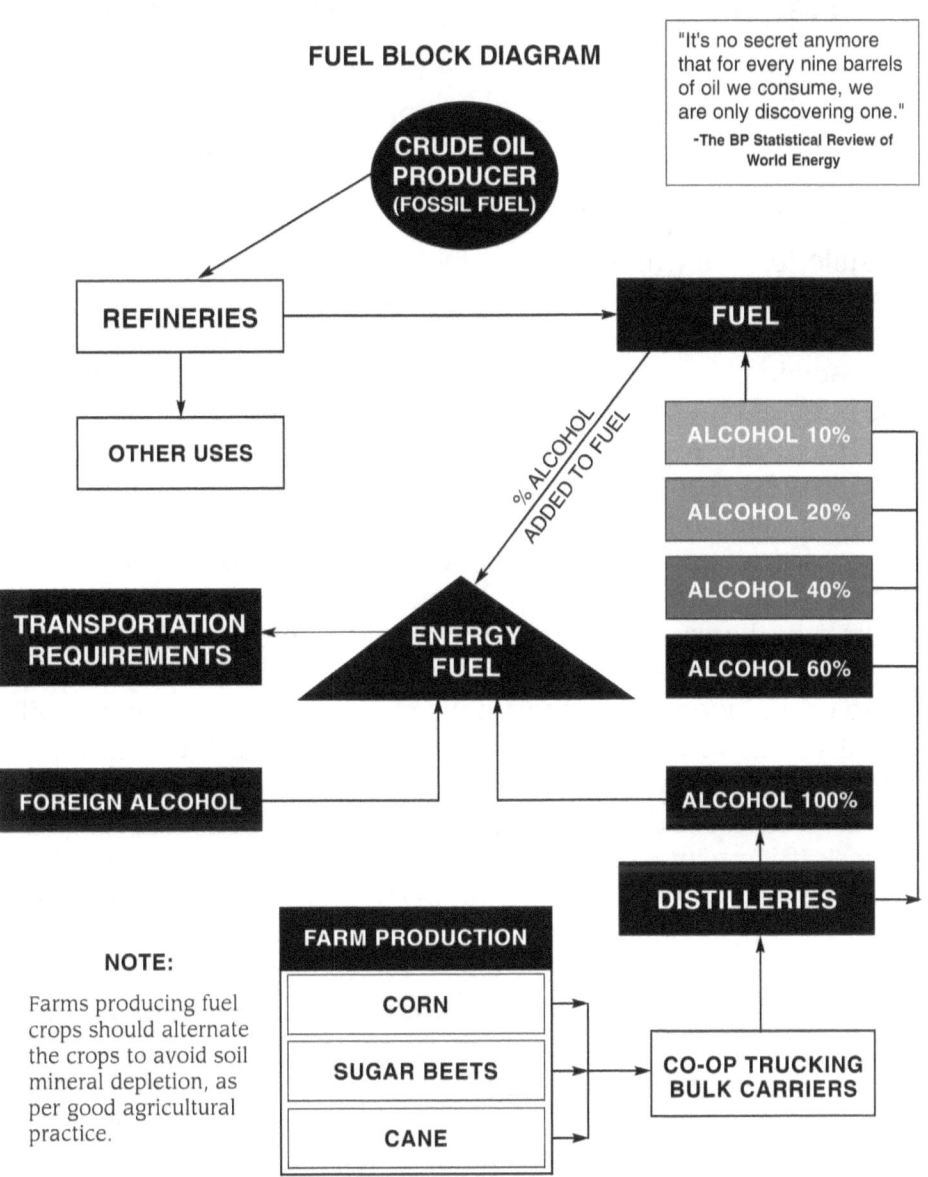

FUEL BLOCK DIAGRAM

"It's no secret anymore that for every nine barrels of oil we consume, we are only discovering one."

-The BP Statistical Review of World Energy

CRUDE OIL PRODUCER (FOSSIL FUEL)

REFINERIES

OTHER USES

FUEL

% ALCOHOL ADDED TO FUEL

ALCOHOL 10%

ALCOHOL 20%

ALCOHOL 40%

ALCOHOL 60%

TRANSPORTATION REQUIREMENTS

ENERGY FUEL

FOREIGN ALCOHOL

ALCOHOL 100%

DISTILLERIES

NOTE:

Farms producing fuel crops should alternate the crops to avoid soil mineral depletion, as per good agricultural practice.

FARM PRODUCTION

CORN

SUGAR BEETS

CANE

CO-OP TRUCKING BULK CARRIERS

THE FUEL FARMER OF THE FUTURE:

The farmers who plant crops for fuel, plant the crops, harvest it and then must transport it to a processing facility. The truck that transports it can be independent or part of a co-op shared among a group of farming people. The harvest-to-fuel process is already in place. We need more (for lack of a better word) distilleries. We will need these fuel farms all over our country so that weather patterns do not interfere with our fuel outputs. The retail distribution (service station) may be located in a station already in place. Or a new one could be set up. The pumps can be painted emerald green to indicate a "green" fuel.

The farmer's compensation can be just the payment for just the crop he produces or he may want to be part of the final process income. I don't know, this is a logistics problem. I don't know if we need fossil fuel producers part of this. If it is needed what I will not want to have happen is: for the giants of fuel to take "the lion's share" of the money. We must not be greedy. Today costs at the pump go way up–profits of fuel suppliers goes into orbit. I won't have that! If it's required the government will float bonds to build the infrastructure to make the idea not a dream, but reality.

Let's consider the benefits. How much CO2 does alcohol produce? If it's way better than for gasoline–we win "big time," in causing less harm to the ozone layer or in creating less smog. It also reduces out dependence upon foreign oil and lowers our debt to foreign nations. If I were President, I would need help in bringing these items to bear. We need positive thinking only and quite a bit of innovative thinking as well. I don't want to hear, "we cannot do this, because … if I do, that person better have a new job lined up! Foreign nations are already using alcohol for fuel. So no one is going to tell me Americans cannot. There is nothing we cannot do. All of the above takes time, yes. However, if we go flat out and do it instead of talking we will make it happen. In the words of all race car drivers, "Those who win, win by keeping the pedal to the metal."

SPACE AND THE NEXT FRONTIER:

Do you remember when President John F. Kennedy said, "We choose to go to the moon, we choose to go to the moon in this decade ..."? Who do you think he entrusted that mission to? Engineers in every field, scientists, astrophysicists, the medical fields of human interaction with space etc. These men and women probably thought, "Oh my God, how are we going to do this? Where do we start?" etc. Then a click was heard, like throwing a big switch, and these great Americans took the challenge in stride (not without problems, of course) ...

And so began the progress of our space technology. Then and now, they were pioneers–a collection of our finest abstract thinkers. Unfortunately today, you rarely hear about our space achievements. I'm sorry that we do not spend more media coverage EDUCATING THE PUBLIC.

What I would like every American to do is, to attend a launch at the Kennedy Space Center and see "man's dream" become a reality. What you see is true reality, not "reality TV" with great sound. By the way, that sound you hear is the voices of Americans, the liberty and freedom to accomplish the seemingly impossible. Those Astronauts we all know and love are a very small part of that mission. There are thousands of Americans that made that launch a reality. Thank you, President Kennedy, for your abstract thinking.

THE NEW FRONTIER—THE WORLD'S OCEANS:

Space was tough, however, the next frontier is much more difficult. Very difficult because we require the acceptance of the world to make it a complete success. That is almost an impossible problem to solve. We can start with the ocean's inhabitants–fish and other ocean species. Over-fishing the world's oceans is an on-going problem.

Starting at home, I would like to see the end of whale hunting—totally! To our north American neighbors, brothers and sisters, please put down your old traditions of whale killing. Throughout American history we have ALTERED (with our consent) our ways of doing things and have done away with old traditions.

I would like to see our territorial waters distances extend out to our Continental Shelf for most of all the preservation of our fishing industry's territory. This comes under the United Nation's Convention on the law of the sea. There is one area I objected to in the UNCLOS II and that was Part XI which related to the mining use of the ocean's seabeds. As I understand it, a new group called I.S.A. (International Seabed Authority) would authorize, or allow, a specific portion of the seabed to be mined and collect a royalty from the company or country mining that specific area. These royalites would be collected and then distributed among all those doing the mining. What that seems to me is very much like, if I was a great author who has a best seller that is making millions of dollars my publisher would distribute the money among all the other authors. Does this portion of the law of the sea sound like America? What is does is eliminate the incentive to find new frontiers.

What I would like to see is, the countries of Canada, Greenland, Denmark, Sweden and all the island countries the Caribbean, South America on the eastern side of the Atlantic set up a 200 mile restricted fishing zone. My reason is that a marine biologist, Mr. B. Worm from Canada, has been studying the "fish harvesting" for the past 50 years. He and other groups who have been studying this have concluded that at the present level of harvest, the world at some point in time, is going to produce the extinction of the following sea life varieties: sharks (used for food), Atlantic Cod, Sturgeon, Pacific Salmon, Red Snapper, Bluefin Tuna, Grouper, Swordfish and many others. What I'm telling you here is not from a disaster novel, IT IS REAL! We, and the world are on a path to a major disaster. When is enough, enough? When we go out to fish and they are truly extinct? We must control (curb) the amount of fish we catch within our waters. All other nations must do the same or these fish will go the way of our American Bison.

Perhaps we could add a small "use tax" for fish per ton caught. 100% of this use tax money received will be set aside for specific areas. The taxes could be used for patrolling these expanded fishing territories; for ocean research in fishing related fields; and as loans to private American companies that set up Fish Hatcheries along our coast lines.

Working side by side, these Fish Hatcheries could be a great supplement to our fish populations in boosting and replenishing the ocean's native stock; whereas, the actual Fish Farms would be used to add a fresh-farmed bounty directly to our tables. The Salmon industry is doing this now and it could be expanded to other types of fish. Together, they would boost our fishing economy and, most of all, aid our *friends from the sea* by giving them time to "go forth and multiply."

One item concerning the ocean, California has laws forbidding dumping of sewage or garbage overboard. All pleasure boats have holding tanks inside for sewage. These tanks return to dockside and are pumped into holding tanks on shore. All ships, including our own, will not pump bilge oils and garbage within the territorial waters. We could set up floating receiving barges for sewage and wastes that take these items to shore for proper disposal or reclamation. Foreign ships will be charged for this service. Sometime in the near future ships of all nations should be required to have these holding tanks. Our oceans are too precious and valuable to destroy.

Now, I don't know if you who are reading this, but understand how great and important the ocean is to all of us. I'll say that again to ALL OF US! Because if we as people of this planet continue to pollute and destroy life forms in the ocean (by eating or other reasons), we may all die. Mankind may not *die right now*, but in our future. I'm not running around like "Chicken Little" and crying, "the sky is falling, the sky is falling,"–no, not at all. What I'm telling you is the ocean gives us life. Not just fish life, but the microscopic plant-like sea creatures known as Phytoplankton supply not only food for millions of fish and whales, but supply us with approximately **50% of the world's oxygen (by most estimates)**. Those wonderful trees and vegetation on earth supply the other 50%. There is much scientific research being done out there on these current subjects. (See National Geographic News–June 7, 2004; and also the website: www.gsfc.nasa.gov/topstory/20020801plankton.)

So if we destroy by damaging the oceans, which everyone on earth is doing (or by denuding our planet of vegetation), the balance may eventually not be enough to support our growing global population. You and I might live to a ripe old age, but future generations may not.

Please take heed in protecting our oceans from pollution and over-fishing. We have two homes in our lifetime ... your first home is a constant (the earth), but the other (where you were born/live) is variable. All of us are tied to the environment called earth. It is our home for at least 80 years if all goes well. Please take care of our first home, the earth. It is a matter of life or death.

THE IUCN AND THE ENVIRONMENT:

*Our rights are being taken away due to UN Mandate!
Every American should know that the U.S.A. is imple-
menting International Policy, which can cause great
harm. This is unnecessary harm to the American citizens. We are paying a major price for allowing the IUCN
(International Union for the Conservation of Nature).*
(The above is my statement *prior* to reading more
about the IUCN initiatives.)

Recently I was given a report found on the internet. It was written by the IUCN. It's topic is Forests Under Fire. **Web Reference:
http://www.iucn.org**

RE: The World Conservation Union's: "Forests Under Fire"

I totally believe in what the IUCN has done around the world,
but not in the U.S.A. However, I have many questions to ask
regarding their report. I don't understand their chart on **Regions
and % of original forest remaining**. They use % (of forest
remaining) as a start from 8,000 years ago. Wow, first thing I'll
say is, that anyone who uses data that far back is asking to pollute the information. How do you know? How would anyone …
you know, the average person? The answer is: you don't know
what you don't know. I use that as my basis when I do not know.
Simple. That type of data will be used by those who truly believe,
like the Sierra Club, who has clearly stated: "we oppose all logging activities–whether on federal, state, provincial, or private
lands–that are environmentally unsustainable …" Or the person
who has no ties to any organization will say, that 8,000 years
ago makes no sense. How do you verify? Why not use 100 years
ago? We still have people alive and we probably have written
documents, photos somewhere. That's much more realistic!
That, perhaps 80% of the population would understand.

My second issue with this chart is: that different nations are bunched together (example Russia and Europe), but you place America with Central America. Why? If you use North America and that includes Canada, that's fine, because Canada and America are quite close in culture. Central America is not. It came under the control of Spain–a different culture. So I'm going to re-arrange the chart for you. I come up with North America has 80 to 85% of it's original forests (a guess). Not too bad, but it can improve. We can always do better.

IUCN: The World Conservation Union's– "Landscapes with People"

IUCN states: *"People are living in most forested land-scapes, each with their individual stories and experiences. Which voices really count when important decisions are made about forests? A landscape approach that includes local people's opinions and behavior means that costs and benefits can be shared fairly between those who directly depend upon the forests for their livelihoods, as well as the wider international community."*

I have a difficult problem trying to understand the words spoken above and the actions taken by IUCN control. The first part is, *Which voices really count when important decisions are made ...?* Yes, their voices were heard all right, the voices of only "environmental power brokers" and the decisions were made at the international member's meeting.* I would guess that the local people's opinions were heard *after* the decisions were locked in concrete. Great going IUCN and in particular the Clinton gang: Bruce Babbitt and his henchman, Michael Dombeck.

I do not know what "the wider International community" means, however I will take a good guess. I'm guessing the "International community" took action against the U.S.A. by closing all logging and scrapping our logging saw mills throughout our country. I believe that we the people, of the U.S.A. get the privilege and honor of paying for wood products from foreign nations.

I read this report that says, we in America, are the greatest caregivers of forests in the world. The other nations that also care are Canada, New Zealand, and Australia. In South America the rain forests must be protected. That's your job IUCN. Go after the ones who are failing. But that's not how the system works. In my estimation, the attack is always on the "good." Take away guns from the innocent. Attack victims, not criminals. Yes, that's how it's done. It follows the playbook.

From what the IUCN report states (North and Central America has retained 75% of original forests), the United States is in great shape, that's comparing (continents) in your own report, if it's true. So why don't you gather all your people and start with the countries who are in "deep poop?" Such as Africa, an almost lost continent with problems so grave that there may not be an African person around in 25 years. Also help Asia (big area to take on). We, in America don't need the IUCN. You understand that this report was probably generated in Gland, Switzerland (IUCN Headquarters) and I believe that is still in Europe. You guys have a lot of work to do in your own back yard. According to your chart 58% of the forests are left in Russia and Europe–you better get cracking!

In the IUCN Report, *Forests Under Fire*, under the heading, "What Are the Threats?" you state that: *"Forest fires perhaps account for 40% of annual global greenhouse emissions in severe fire years. When they burn, forests produce a double negative effect on the climate as they no longer absorb carbon dioxide, but release it and significantly contribute to global warming."* As I read this, I noticed someone used a number again, 40% and preceded it with the word PERHAPS. Perhaps is uncertainty or possibility, maybe. O.K. so what we have again is a percent from 20% to 60%? You don't know? Now what is really scary is the word SIGNIFICANTLY. That itself is very serious. So, if I get this truly straight, we would prefer NO FOREST FIRES, CORRECT? If we can agree about forest fires not being good for our environment. Then I must ask why a forest service person when asked if we are to maintain our natural resources, would you thin out the forest and remove the dead foliage or burn? The answer was, "let it burn." Now I would ask, the information I'm reading sounds very good to me: "to sustain our forests," that's perfect. Is the material before me written by your organization (IUCN), a propaganda message? Because there seems to me to be a real major disconnect between what is written and what is done. I call this a political statement. Believe what I say, but do not ask why I do nothing.

So from my viewpoint, the IUCN is, by deed, contributing to global warming. By not allowing forest groups (these people are the doers not the talkers) to go into areas that NEED cleaning up, to remove trees down, clean up. You know, it's called common sense. No, we don't seem to want to do that, lawsuits by the score. What is your game? I believe in ecosystem management. How can I not?

What are the threats? The IUCN says, *"All countries and communities are grappling with the challenge of meeting growing demands for food, clean water, health and employment."* What do you mean ALL? I see, as an American, two major threats. At the top of the list is employment. Since the beginnings of IUCN policies into our forests, Americans have lost 10,000 or more jobs. Just how big are the forest people and the jobs that rely on timber? It's a guess, I don't know! Of course, neither do we know, just how many jobs have been *gained* in the areas of environmental growth and the "sustainable forestry ecosystem" support and research. I would venture to guess that more than 10,000 jobs have been gained in the past 50 years.

What I am real worried about the possibility of radical groups within the NGO (Non-Governmental Association) who have shown and almost religious and fanatical approach for their cause. That worries me "big time."

*IUCN meets every four years at the World Conservation Congress–the Union's General Assembly–to expresss their views, guide the Union's policy and approve its program. The last Congress was held in Bangkok, Thailand in November 2004).

Look at our Middle Eastern problems–religious and fanatical approach to connect their point of view. Not good. First of all, their approach is not in the Koran, the holy book of the Muslims. What we have here are groups of these fanatics who wish to interpret the holy words into their idealistic doctrine. First of all, the Koran teaches (as does the Bible), do not kill children or others. A holy war, we keep hearing about, refers to the faith of Islam being attacked. That is also not true.

So we return to the fanatical NGOs. Do you remember how even the loving guy, a player in the anti-abortion group, decided to become the returning Christ to earth to strike down sinners? So in his "goodness" blew up an abortion clinic. The same type of person showed the world by bombing the Olympics. I call him and others who approach and use their ideas as a "god-like position." Those are what I call fanatics. You also remember the Jim Jones' group? Nice going fanatics of the world! So we keep Eric Rudolph and Terry Nichols alive and well, while we forget the inner city people whose major crime is being poor.

Of course health has been a long-standing problem in the U.S.A. The escalation of illegals entering our country has placed a major drain on our health system. They come and use our health care system, but do not pay. The health care system then asks for more money from our county or state to fill in their loss. The balance comes from cost increases to pay the difference.

More facts IUCN presents:

The Atlantic cod fisheries are almost extinct. That is not a new fact. It started a long time ago. Fishing ships with mile long and mile and a half long nets sweeping over the ocean. Yeah, I remember, I was on my way to Denmark and I stopped in Portland, Maine. What a great place! I asked the YMCA lady where I could get a great lobster dinner. She said, "Boones." (I believe the time frame was about 1968.) I went out on the balcony to see the lobster pens and view the beautiful ocean. There were a group of fishermen outside and they told me how far they had to travel to get a good catch of fish. The fish on our coastline are being over-fished. I saw large fishing vessels from nations far away when I went out to sea in my boat.

So over-fishing has been with us for a very long time, nothing new again. I remember a study by a Canadian marine biologist who apparently has tracked the fish in the oceans for over 50 years. So the point is, why don't I know about any changes? What I would love to know is what the IUCN has done in trying to change the loss of fish species, say in the last ten years, other than map the species decline.

I am totally behind the IUCN on their energy use ideas. I have designed and built solar panels mainly for hot water heating in homes and pools. You cannot beat the benefits it gives you. I would like to see all homes be fitted with a minimum of 2kw electrical solar cells that will feed into the main (electrical) grid. (These solar, photovoltaic, cells would be made by manufacturing groups in the USA only.) These 2kw units will produce about 480kw per month in California. That would cost you about $60 per month. However, by feeding the power back to the grid, the cost to you per month is zero.

Wind energy is used in California "big time." Altamont Pass has 200-500(?) wind energy units now in use. Yet they produce only 1.5% of California's usage (2004 stats).

I believe in the use of nuclear energy. I understand the benefits and the downfalls. If we always look at the past in any new technology, you will find problems. However, nuclear power is quite old by "new" standards. It's sixty years old and the U.S.A. has made incredible advances in nuclear engines powering ships and submarines. The advancements are understanding the engineering problems and solving them. We have made great leaps forward.

WORLD POPULATION AND MAN'S PROGRESS:

The world's MAIN problem has never been brought to the top of the list of problems. I'm just about to step into the "biggest puddle of shit." It's called *population*. Now if we can sit down and view this without emotional responses, religious outcries, human rights problems and a large host of other responses, over population is the planet Earth's doomsday clock. Now, man over the last 5,000 years has found a way to reduce the population. It's called war against anyone and I mean anyone. You see it today in Iraq. The terrorists call themselves people of the Islamic faith. That's a lie. It sounds great to the children and others who follow their ideals Terrorist ideals are not the true faith of the Muslim people. They claim they are waging a war against the non-believer–the *infidels*. Well, that is so false it's almost unbelievable. The Koran does not teach anyone to kill. In fact, how do they justify the mass killings of (largely Kurdish Sunni Islams) Muslims?

The IUCN literature speaks of the population increases, that's all. They have no solution (that they mention) to the problem. What my main problem with the IUCN is its sustainable meeting–meetings that go on forever. They have a staff of 1,000 persons, world-wide 350 "experts," 70 member states, over 100 government agencies, 800 NGOs (Non-governmental agencies), and over 10,000 scientists and "experts." I look at all those people and wonder, What a monster of a bureaucracy!"

I have seen the results of IUCN work in foreign lands and it is very good. They still have a major problem with population! To date, I have not seen any real progress within the U.S.A. of your policies. However, I have seen the destruction of our forests. You speak reverently of the about the North Atlantic cod fisheries, that put 30,000 Canadians out of work and ruined the economies of 700 communities. They never mention the Canadian government policy to have government exterminations to erase the Arctic Wolves. Nor do they concern themselves about the losses in the United States. What I have learned working with high tech companies is: you always have a group of people who *only talk*. The other group, much smaller, is the one who *does things*. The last group of people, small in number, are those with the *I don't care attitude!*

ENERGY SOLUTIONS–ALL WILL BE POLICY:

1. ALL new homes to have a minimum of a 2kw solar electrical panel. All power grid suppliers to allow inter-connection agreements. Owners or builders can increase the size of the panel, power as required.

2. Any permits for remodeling of existing homes could at this time add the solar grid panel(s).

3. All commercial, industrial and agricultural buildings could add solar panels for their particular uses.

All of the above will have a tremendous impact on all the power grids by saving on fossil fuel, natural gas, propane and perhaps on hydro which is great. (However during certain times we pump too much water and that can affect some of the fish life.)

We can and should continue to use wind generators, ocean power generators, and the use of solar concentrators to create steam and in turn drive steam turbines for electricity. We can support the power grids with the use of these solar panels. This will be a major change, power producers will not have to build more power stations, which are VERY expensive. We will all help out our environment and, in the long run, our pocketbooks.

4. All A.C. units on new homes to have a rating of 15 seer (Current regulations are at 13 seer). Regulations of 18 seer should be required in regions of severe high temperatures. (such as in Arizona, New Mexico and some parts of Texas). All replacement units will also follow the same, unless major installation problems occur.

5. All gas heating units (furnaces) shall have an efficiency of rating 93-96%. These furnaces are called Condensing Furnaces.

6. Home locations must be better designed to take advantage of N-S configuration (solar orientation facing south). North-facing walls should have minimum windows, with south windows large and west windows medium-large. However, extended overhangs could help with too much sun on the windows during the summer months.

For more information on this, see **Energy Star** rated homes ...
RESNET (Residential Energy Services Network)
Ratings provides a relative energy use index called the HERS Index–a HERS Index of 100 represents the energy use of the "American Standard Building" and an Index of 0 (zero) indicates that the Proposed Building uses no net purchased energy (a Zero Energy Building). A set of Rated Recommendations for cost-effective improvements that can be achieved by the Rated Building is also produced. See website: natresnet.org.

As you can see the closer to zero we get the more efficient the home. The concept is called "Zero Energy Building (ZEB)." The current regulations for this are due for updating from the 2005 building codes to new codes for 2008. Only one house in the United States has demonstrated 12 months of data showing net-zero-energy performance; that house, located in Wheat Ridge, Colorado and was built by Metro Denver Habitat for Humanity, with help from NREL (National Renewable Energy Laboratory) engineers. This ZEB concept has been adopted completely in the United Kingdom. Their government has announced an "ambitious plan" to build all new homes with zero energy building by 2016! See Wikipedia.org–Zero Energy Building.

So as I see it, energy ratings for homes in America should be around 50 on that scale. That should be our goal and we have proved it is doable with help from the NREL.

Homes should be designed to bring into the home natural light. Especially in rooms with no outside walls, use skylights to bring in light and thus cut down the use of electric light. Think of all the savings in America, if all bathrooms used only natural light during the day time.

This concept of using natural light (his term: *organic architecture*) is pure Frank Lloyd Wright, my mentor ... By studying his designs at 16 through 17 years of age, I designed my own home when I was seventeen. It is very energy efficient.

7. All new homes to have at least 80% lighting that is of the Fluorescent type. Most of these lights give you a 75% savings on watts alone, plus the benefit of not giving off 90% of the heat that incandescents produce. Their longevity alone is a reason for their usage.

8. All new homes to have a hot water recirculation system. This is most imperative! It saves untold loss of pure water that goes directly into the grey water waste system without any use of the water. It also saves energy–the energy that was used in heating the water.

This is what I use. It's 14 years old and still works beautifully: a recirculator made by FASCO Industries, Inc. A 1/100 HP pump rated at 250 F. It's a sealess pump, magnetic drive. It uses almost no electrical power to run. You plug it in to a standard timer that you can control by "time your lifestyle." Mine has been very faithful to me over 14 years. You can use bigger pumps, but for what? This pump, when installed, will deliver 3 gpm, but the pump intake is the return from your hot water line, such as your lavatory or sink. This pump does not supply you the actual water, your std. line does that. This pump only returns the unused hot water to the water heater.

One major problem in developer/builders is they rarely *exceed* energy efficiency regulations in building a home. We must do better because the people who live in that home will pay for that lack of efficiency for a very long time. Some things can be done to make it better, but if a home is poorly designed, you may be out of luck. Each home a developer/builder brings to the Planning Department should have, in writing, the energy rating of that home. Then add the appliance ratings separately. Before the home is passed to the happy new owner, an independent, usually state-sanctioned with instruments of the trade, should review the home site. These experts are really great in what they do. Many builders or developers do not like their approach to finding faults. What they find, that needs fixing to codes, is written down and signed by that person who did the inspection. Copies of the report are sent to the state/county agencies, to the builder developer, and to the owner to be.

The building inspector that comes from the county agency, a standard inspector, is not versed in all aspects of home construction. However, these independents have specific licenses and are like, say for an example, the Licensed Land Surveyor." They are experts, *real experts*.

My father, later in life, worked as a building inspector for the cities of Fremont and Dublin, California. My dad was tough and he always wanted to do the right thing in his life and his job. He told me that many inspectors are called "curb-side inspectors"—inspecting from the curb sitting in their car.

LAWYERS AND POLITICIANS:

You may have noticed how hard I am on lawyers and politicians. Well, they are pretty closely related. I have attacked them as a group and perhaps that is unfair. There are sure to be some good ones who believe in America. Totally believe–not by simply saying I am an American and wearing that cute little American flag over their heart. But by showing us by giving us laws that punish crime and not punish the victims of the crime!

Have you noticed that every four years the same topics come up with the same results–no real actions taken? What has happened to the art of compromise? The problems face all of us not just the Democrats or Republicans. You and I have heard for the last 25 to 35 years that the government was going to do the following:

1. Reduce crime, yeah, that sure happened.
2. More severe penalties for criminals–we release criminals now
3. Reduce drug use in America–In general, we just see a change in the popular drug in current use.
4. Health Care for all Americans–instead we give free health care to illegals
5. More jobs for Americans–instead we send our companies and factories to other nations and hire other nationalities to do our jobs here. We then buy raw materials that we already have here within America from other countries. Wake up America!
6. Election reforms–each time that happens we get screwed.
7. Contribution reforms–it means one party is not getting that extra $50 million dollars for their "tribal war chest. " Each tribe Democrat or Republican spend most of the time fighting each other and very little time telling you what they believe and support. They have forgotten what we are needing to hear to decide upon whom to vote. Or are we really such sheep now that all we need is their political label or religion to decide?
8. Tax Reforms–our government is about to be more corrupted. Become alert–reform means change and should only mean for the better of all. I ask better for whom?

One obvious example is in our tax codes. Do our current tax codes speak of banks in foreign nations or of offshore banking? The Swiss Banks, the Cayman Islands and perhaps many more locations are "havens" set up to give Americans a way to evade the tax laws of income. Does offshore banking help the American government have enough (income tax) money for the many aids and protections that we expect it to do for us? Does the word "loophole" come to mind here? Does offshore banking include money placed there by other nations for our lobbyist groups, legislative bribe money, etc.? The IRS laws of *tax evasion*, I think they should apply here. Where are the real "tax reforms?" Is there anyone honest enough in government to apply or create such tax reforms?

You know the motto of Missouri–the *"show me state."* I love those mottos, they sound old time like our founding fathers or something. While I'm talking about Missouri, I'll say I'm ashamed of you because the Missourians that I know do not allow statements and promises by government incumbents to slip by without a challenge. Perhaps you should change your motto now. Have your elected officials actually *showed you* what they said they would do? (This also applies to all the other states as well.) I am also guilty for our lack of control over elected leaders.

TRAIL BLAZERS:

Our culture has been led by what I call Trail Blazers or Pioneers. These people led by example. They set forth into an unknown territory and were sure that there was something to discover, somewhere new to go. Once they found what they were after, they relied upon the next group of people, the masters of engineering to say, "Let's lay the tracks or roads here. These roads and tracks are followed today by all of us who take these things for granted.

Our civilization relies upon and runs on that track. However to keep this, means moving forward, requiring vast amounts of work by others to maintain and "so to speak, grease the wheels of progress." Sooner or later that engine of progress slows or stops and every one of us wonders, "what happened?" We stand around until someone steps forward to get the engine running once again.

I feel like that I am that sort of person, because my life is already planned–it is inescapable. I must continue on to see my journey's end. I look at our vast lands in the Midwest region–farms that have been in existence for so many generations. The main fault our Midwest has is a lack of water. Farmers depend upon Mother Nature to care for us and our farms. I have often wondered what would happen if we had our Army Corps of Engineers tap into the great Mississippi River that flows south to the ocean's gulf. If we were to run a massive underground pipe west from the river to the Midwest, this could solve some of the problems of drought. This main water line could follow the railroad lines and be tapped into at different locations along the way to water crops and livestock. Such a pipeline may also help to relieve areas of massive flooding along its banks and in the delta during high rain conditions. During these periods of high rain fall some of the water could be diverted to fill reservoirs or other holding facilities in those drought-ridden areas for emergency usage. Once filled, these reservoirs could be used also for recreation.

Like Mono Lake, at no time should this flow of water be destructive to or harm wildlife and should maintain a healthy flow in the Mississippi.

WATER RECLAMATION (MANDATORY):

I believe we *must* reclaim most of all of our grey water. I would like to see at least 80% reclamation of grey water. Look at Las Vegas as a prime example of needed water reclamation. Its beautiful hotels with massive fountains. etc. The water useage is enormous. The reclaimed water would be pumped for usage again in all the landscaping and all the fountain uses in the whole area. Perhaps even used in the laundering of the massive amounts of bedding used daily. Users will pay, by meter a small fee for the amount of water used.

The technology is already in place. We need to find locations to build reclamation facilities, usually next to sewage disposal plants. Greywater can be processed and be reused for irrigation for exterior landscapes. It would not be used for household use, such as drinking and bathing. Underground lines for standard water and power would now carry an additional line to each home and building. Right of ways are already in place.

We are running out of water at our present growth rate. Water is gold!

WATER SOLUTIONS:

The diagram that follows, shows us two problems that we currently just live with and how they may be altered to improve these situations.

Problem One: Flooding along our great Mississippi River
Problem Two: Droughts throughout our farm and ranch lands

These two problems occur almost every year and they destroy millions (billions?) of dollars in crops, homes and destroy American lives and dreams!

So off I go to speak to the local townspeople about flooding and droughts throughout our county. Well, I am disapointed in the responses I received. Some said, "people should just move. I can't help those people, I have problems of my own to think about. There's nothing I can do. One person said they were sorry about the situation. (survey dated Oct 27, 2007). We are truly forgetting what it is to be American, what it is to care about one another. We have forgotten each other and our culture has been affected by this lack of caring.

Well, I care. So you see, my plan of harnessing the mighty Mississippi and reducing the flow of water, or better yet, truly controlling the flow of the water south during high rain conditions may be a solution to both of these problems.Re-directing the high water to the east and to the west of the Mississippi into some type of reservoir system, could help farms in times of drought. What we can do is take the enormous force of nature and use it for our own benefit.

People have told me that these programs I recommend will take lots of money, but in the final result they will save lots of expense in rebuilding and in lost crop revenues. I'm sure that we could raise a lot of that money. Just think, Americans spent over 1.5 billion dollars on Halloween alone this past year. Let's put things in America into the proper perspective.

My plan for better water usage and flood control is shown below:

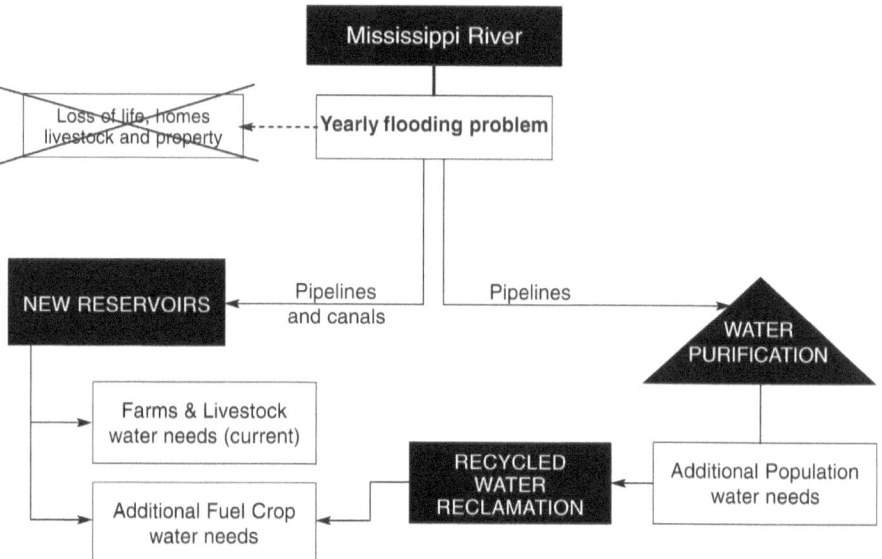

PREVENTION OF THE LOSS OF OUR FARMS AND RANCHES:

A Mandatory Program

Today our farms and ranches are disappearing, due to taxes; inability to pay the bills overdue to banks; crop losses do to weather conditions; but mostly due to development. Developers of everything pay off politicians and city councils in rural areas; cash-strapped county governments approve development projects to swell their city coffers and cover county budget shortfalls. In California some of the greatest most fertile soil on earth is found in the Central Valley. I have seen in the last ten years housing projects that exceed many thousands or more and many strip malls to support them. The above are just some of the examples of how our farm lands are being taken over for whatever reason.

We **must** protect our farm and ranch lands from other uses throughout our country from sea to sea. I think I know how we can do this! First, let me ask you this: if we continue at the current rate of farm and ranch land loss, at what point do we say, "enough is enough?" "Do we want to be waiting in lines to buy bread because the bread is made in only one part of our country? Or worse, would you put your faith in foreign nations to feed us by importing our food? One of America's greatest strengths is our ability to feed us and still support many other nations. We, as Americans, need to understand that we cannot lose any more of our precious farm and ranch land. If we do, we will pay for it with much higher food bills, food with less quality and less variety of foods.

Now, I'm asking myself, why should I worry about waiting in line for food? My life is short and I won't ever see those kind of food shortages. However, I cannot think like that. My parents and all my grandparents taught me not to think like that. So I think in the future and have to go forward to "fix it." This is what I would do. Many of our past presidents have set aside land for our National Forests, National Parks, wildlife preserves and other protected areas in our country. What I want is this ... All lands (over a specific size) that are now used for agriculture, ranch lands and any land that supplies us with food products will be considered a "National Agricultural Preserve." The exception to the current policy would include that these National Agricultural Preserves not be owned nor managed by the federal or state governments. This land will be owned exclusively by the present owner as stated in the deed. If that owner wants to sell his land, said land must be sold to a new farmer ONLY. Under the main blanket of a National Agricultural Preserve, under no condition must the said land be encroached upon by anyone. When there is a death in the family of a farm or active ranch owner, within the farmer's property NO DEATH TAXES will be permitted. Family members will be permitted to continue to operate the land. The only property taxes permitted are those placed upon the home itself. Farm land will be non-taxable as long as it is in some kind of *active agricultural use*. I also include ranch lands and tree farms in this category. These lands must be used for agriculture as the "primary source of income for the property owner" for it to qualify for this program.

Farmers and ranchers know how to bring their products to the market. The government cannot be micro-managing agricultural lands. This is not the government's place. No government subsidies will be handed out to pay farmers NOT to plant crops. Perhaps the farmer may want to use his land to plant "fuel-based" crops instead.

On agricultural lands that are currently non-productive, perhaps we should be planting crops for fuel use. If we have an over abundance of certain crops that would end up in warehouse storage and non-use, perhaps we should convert them to crops for fuel use also.

What I'm attempting to do here is to insure the survivability of our food and agriculture producing Americans. They are at a grave risk today. (Read more: *Animal, Vegetable, Miracle* by Barbara Kingsolver). I keep hearing the same old song about what will we leave our children and the future of their children. I've mostly heard about global warming and that's another whole topic. I have never heard anyone speak out or give any new solutions to solve any other problems and certainly not reforms in our food supply and marketing practices. Give our farmers and ranchers room and they will produce. They have been doing it generation after generation.

ON AMERICAN INDUSTRY:

The dream I have of America is in our people. They have put on the "idle," waiting for the industrialists to put faith once again into the people of the greatest country. To once again turn on the switch to unleash the awesome power of American industry. We probably have thousand of buildings standing still (empty), ready to rise to the sound of manufacturing. I believe I know why we go offshore–labor costs. However, have our great (franchise chains), such as Sears, Maytag, the appliance manufacturer, WalMart, K-Mart, the general merchandise and clothing outlets, gone offshore? I wonder where my wife bought my underwear from–I hope she didn't buy it from a foreign country. That's too close to my heart–I'm good, I'm good–made in the U.S.A.

I don't know what it would take to have these major retail stores begin to set up manufacturing facilities here. What I'm suggesting is, what if our government bought up these buildings and leased them back to the retail stores? Now these retail stores could set up manufacturing of goods, then distribute them with their name brand, etc. I do not know the actual cost difference between U.S.A-made and foreign-made goods. I always attempt to buy American. The reason is I have no idea as to what it costs us overall. The cost of paying Americans not working? Where does that money come from? The counties or states could give tax relief to these manufacturing companies. The people employed will be taxed for income. They will also use their spendable money to buy products within their town.

I truly do not know very much about economics. However, Grandfather Mailho always said, "Money must always be in motion or the town or city will come to a halt." How true that is.

In our northwest our lumber industries have stopped. People are unemployed. Towns may become like years ago–ghost towns. The state will take a hit and crime will rise. Must I say more?

Advertising costs are not free–automobile manufacturing uses a lot of advertising. Now add in transportation costs. I know the cost difference between the WalMart brand, called "Sam's Choice," and say Post or Kelloggs brand, which is very good. A big difference in price. I will always buy American if I have a choice.

AMERICAN MANUFACTURING (TO DO REQUEST):

I would like to see American manufacturing companies in all fields, to financially support "mentoring" (on-the-job training). Within their field of expertise, each company could designate current experts in their company to mentor new employees. I'm sure that in return, the new employee could sign a contract saying that if he/she completes this mentoring program satisfactorily and becomes a permanent employee that they must give a minimum of one year of service in that company's employ. This could all be in a signed agreement before taking on a mentored position. What this program will do is take book knowledge and apply it to real world use. The question always asked on an application for employment is: "What experience do you have?" Perhaps none is needed if that company is willing to mentor a new employee.

The government could even give tax breaks to companies complying with this effort. Not only will American manufacturing get a boost in qualified employees, but they will be helping put Americans back to work. (No illegals)! If this does not happen, the we, the people, pay the government to support these people through welfare and unemployment entitlements.

CRUISE SHIP PROBLEMS (TO DO REQUEST):

Have you noticed over the last eight years, the problems of American tourists aboard cruise ships? Most of these ships are built in Germany, Norway or Italy. The ships are registered in foreign countries, the employees may be from foreign countries, often from third world countries. Also crime is a problem within International Waters. So one of the problems we have is, who do you go to when problems arise? The U.S. government cannot interfere, so perhaps you go to Interpol. Do you understand what a barrel of worms that is?

The "cruise ships" in the U.S.A. built years ago became obsolete when Howard Hughs showed us the world and the ways of the future. The American public became more "hurry up, hurry up," so we ended a great era of cruise ship building. Ship building in America now consists of military applications. Calling all "wanabes" like Henry J. Kaiser, I have a job that fits your style. Let's build cruise ships once again. However, these cruise ship babies can really move. How would you like to go to Hawaii or Europe in less than three days? Furthermore, let's not be packed in like sardines, or eat pre-packaged foods, or watch movies that you've already seen many times. You get on and off like a herd of sheep. Oh yeah, I like that!

Now this ship is not new, in fact it is quite old–built in 1952. A man by the name of William Francis Gibbs was the brain child of this ship. I consider him to be one of the greatest nautical engineers of his time. He designed a cruise liner that could be changed into a troop carrier. The ship's name, *The United States*.* What else could it be named? This beautiful ship was designed with the idea of function first, form last. It's form is very beautiful and a sight to behold. Driven by four props and 241,000 horsepower engines, she can reach speeds up to 43 knots (about 50mph).

My idea is that since we have many new power plants available, I would choose nuclear power, clean and it does not require us to buy oil. I figured we would need about 80,000 shaft H.P to cruise even faster at 60 to 65mph (with a flank speed some-where over 70mph). Now I'm using mph instead of nautical miles because it is easier for people to relate to. All of these cruise liners could be based on *The United States*, built and registered in the U.S., manned and staffed with American crew members. Many Americans would be once again drawn to using ships as transportation to and from places. Especially due to the shorter travel times.

*www.ssunitedstates.org/theship

SHIP BUILDING–Past and Future

Do you have any idea what it takes to build a ship? When I was very young, my Grandfather took me to the ship yards. I believe they were in Alameda, California. I watched the "Liberty" ships being built and assembled. I remember very large portions of the ship's sections being transported overhead by large cranes into their final positions. I asked my Grandfather if that is the way ships were always built. He said, "Not always, Kaiser's engineers designed the ships so they could be built in sections in different buildings. Then they can be moved into position and assembled as needed. It's called pre-fab."

> Shipbuilding on the West Coast is currently done by **General Dynamics NASSCO** in San Diego (one of three marine operations in the US) employs over 4,600 people in their operation.

He also said that they are building 20-25 ships per month and that most of the workers were women. "Grandpa, I said, "I didn't know that girls could build boats." "Yes, and they can and they also build planes, trucks, and cars," he answered.

"Grandpa, why isn't my mom building ships?" I asked. "She is a teacher and that's also important," he replied. "Your Grandmother is building pies. Do you want your Grandmother to build ships or pies?" "Oh, pies, Grandpa!" I exclaimed. At an early age I learned that "girls" can do everything (I was about seven at the time).

When you take on a large project like shipbuilding, you require a vast amount of resources, which means jobs. I would encourage the U.S. to build more ships and other large scale projects, using only materials and resources from the U.S.A. If industries that were used earlier were shut down, I would like to see them reopened, whenever possible, as F.D.R. would do.

I read, some years ago, a book called, *Naval Battles* (or something like that) about Admiral Yamamoto (Fleet Admiral during WWII) from Japan. He was educated at Harvard University (1919–1921). He once said something like, "I lived in America and went to college there and saw the enormous might of American industry." Now, why is it that an outsider, born in Japan, and very loyal to his country sees America in those terms, where our leadership (if one can call it that) seems to be engrossed in non-important

> – 1942 –
> US Maritime Commission contracted with Kaiser's Oregon Shipbuilding and Bethlehem-Fairfield Shipyard to build the new emergency cargo ships that would make up the "Liberty Fleet."

projects with a "don't give a shit attitude?" We, the people, seem to be preoccupied with in-fighting between the two major political parties. Nothing other than that is important. Every four years that in-fighting begins again and all the programs that each side proposes they "will accomplish." The goals are not reached and have not happened in the past 30 years. Too much Republican and Democrat and too little concern over what America really needs. Congress always comes up with, "We don't have the money." They never tell you how much tax money was spent on "pork projects." Most of these projects do not help the people. (Who allowed the money to be spent for the give away program on the search for some mystical creature in some lake or swamp to the tune of some $25 million dollars?–Televised: Oct. 7, 2007)

I was just thinking, hmm ... is it in the Presidential powers to evoke an Executive Order to give our Legislative Branch of government a vacation for about 335 days? (Just kidding).

MARCH 4th, 1789—CONSTITUTION DAY
A New Commemorative Day

I would like to propose a new Commemorative Day to be added to our calendar– March 4th as **Constitution Day**. On that day in 1789, our fore-fathers gave us a timetable for the start of the government under our new Constitution. And by May 29, 1790 all of the thirteen

ORIGINAL THIRTEEN STATES SIGNED THE CONSTITUTION	
Date Ratified	**State**
1 December 7, 1787	Delaware
2 December 12, 1787	Pennsylvania
3 December 18, 1787	New Jersey
4 January 2, 1788	Georgia
5 January 9, 1788	Connecticut
6 February 6, 1788	Massachusetts
7 April 28, 1788	Maryland
8 May 23, 1788	South Carolina
9 June 21, 1788	New Hampshire
10 June 25, 1788	Virginia
11 July 26, 1788	New York
12 November 21, 1789	North Carolina
13 May 29, 1790	Rhode Island

original states had ratified the Constitution. (The **Bill of Rights, the first ten Amendments**, were added to the Constitution in December 1791). The Constitution now consists of a preamble, the seven original articles, twenty-seven amendments, and a paragraph certifying its enactment by the constitutional convention.

What I would like to see is, every American vote. Americans, use the greatest gift given to you and you alone–the right to vote, privately, as you wish. When you vote, you are American no one can take that away from you (as was done in our past). Americans were killed on their way to the polling booths– remember that! You and I live in the shadows of those men who gave us so much, do not fail them. Our Constitution gave us the greatest level playing field. Whether you are a person on Social Security, like me, or a multi-billionaire like Bill Gates–we both get one vote. By exercising our right to vote we are shaping America's tomorrow. Be a part of this great nation, learn about candidates and issues, and VOTE!

Citizens taking part in our government:

You may say that your parents told you that governmental service is a dirty business. Yes, I've heard it all too! But please remember that if you do not vote, we fall back into the 1700's where Kings and Queens and an elite few ruled all. If today we have politics run by families who have taken power … Pardon me, but they did not take power from us, we gave it to them by doing nothing. If you don't like what's going on, get involved. *We have far better candidates to choose from, but it is up to us to learn about them enough to elect them.* Laziness, on our part, and name recognition on the part of the elected now are the deciding factors that get the next President or Senator elected–because we have not taken the time to actually research the alternatives. Wake up America!

There are millions of great individuals out there who have worked in many professional fields. They have physically worked at his or her profession. These are great, honest people that we no longer have in our government. We need to figure out a way to get them elected. They speak from their heart and would take office to work for the American people and not just for their political party. I may be wrong about ALL of our elected government officials and personnel. I'm sure there are SOME(?) good and honest ones who truly try to make their voice heard for the good of the people of America and not their own personal agenda.

WOMEN AS CABINET MEMBERS:

Someone asked me once, who would you place in position as Cabinet Members if you were President? My thoughts are that out of the 15 Cabinet positions, I would appoint 11 of them women. I would place men in the positions of Homeland Security, Veteran's Affairs, and Attorney General. Why so many women? The answer is that women are far better at many of these jobs, are stronger and have more power. If they are given the chance, they "can do anything."

I learned that very early in my life. Women, a great percentage of them, have the ability to organize, how labor is not equally shared, how to manage money and are very concerned about family. They learned about food, how it is processed, and where it comes from. Health issues and Education are paramount in women's minds. Not only for themselves, but for all American's welfare. They are also concerned with the cost of energy and how it affects their lives and how that reflects back into the direction of home management. Their strengths are hidden because of their compassion and caring nature, but do not cross the line and really anger them. Females of the species can and will protect their young with violence if provoked.

Question: What do I think of Hilary Clinton as President?

Answer: I don't!

We, as Americans, have not really seen who she is. We have seen her political life and the Whitewater fiasco. Her friend was sent to prison for not testifying. I see too many skeletons in her closets to trust her with anything. I believe her only purpose is to continue the Clinton legacy. What does that have to do with America's slide into third world status? She has no plans–at least no plans saying how she plans to fix problems. She is also under the umbrella of Clinton's "family value ideals." Reduce the deficit by eliminating the military?

We have some women within our government who may make good cabinet seat members, however, I do not know them. Most of all I would prefer people who are real professionals, who have in their working life have worked in the field to which cabinet post I would appoint them to. An example would be: For the

Secretary of Agriculture, I would like to see someone with management experience who has owned and operated farms with hands on application. A woman who knows what it takes to make our agricultural system run more smoothly and efficiently. I know there are many women out there who have worked in one of those cabinet fields within the private sector. That's the women I would want to consider for these positions. When you go to a dentist, would you want a Dr. of Dentistry or a Farrier to pull a tooth? Both could do the job, which would you choose?

I do think it is time for us to turn over our highest seats of office to our women. Indirectly, many of them have been in control, but most of us would not admit it. I have faith in them to once again return to the ideals of our founding fathers. I could call them the "founding mothers" of this nation of greatness.

I want to tell you something I have never said to anyone nor wrote down, before now. In my life I have accomplished many great achievements, much of it not within these papers. What I want you to know is that I cannot take credit for all of it. (Now my failures are mine–totally mine.) Everything I have done is credited to my teachers, parents, grandparents, and my adopted grandparents. My mentors, Colin Howen, Dr. Benzine, Frank Lloyd Wright, Lynn Brewer (who allowed me to run free), Ron Plescia, R. Cory and hundreds more. They also are responsible for who I am today and what I accomplished in my life. The gift they gave me can never be repaid.

My grandfather once told me that when you learn something, pass the knowledge on to someone else–that way when you teach others and knowledge is not forgotten. So, everything I've done is the total sum of each and every one of them.

"Thank You for reading this" does not truly express the depth of my feelings.

To reach Bob Mailho, please write:

The American Party
P.O. Box 746
Okahumpka, FL 34762

978-0-595-52090-9
0-595-52090-1

www.ingramcontent.com/pod-product-compliance
Lightning Source LLC
Chambersburg PA
CBHW051433280526
45785CB00003B/1272